SAMUEL CUNARD

NOVA SCOTIA'S MASTER OF THE NORTH ATLANTIC

JOHN BOILEAU

Formac Publishing Company Limited
Halifax

To my granddaughters — Sophie, Kya, Emma and Zoë — and their futures, which will encompass technologies not yet imagined.

Also by John Boileau:

Fastest in the World: The Saga of Canada's Revolutionary Hydrofoils (2004)
Half-Hearted Enemies: Nova Scotia, New England and the War of 1812 (2005)
Valiant Hearts: Atlantic Canada and the Victoria Cross (2005)
Consulting Editor:
A Century of Service: Canada's Armed Forces from the Boer War to East Timor (2000)
Contributing Writer:
The Haligonians: 100 Fascinating Lives from the Halifax Region (2005)

Formac Publishing Company Limited recognizes the support of the Province of Nova Scotia through the Department of Tourism, Culture and Heritage. We acknowledge the financial support of the Government of Canada through the Book Publishing Industry Development Program (BPIDP) for our publishing activities.

Formac Publishing Company Limited acknowledges the support of the Canada Council for the Arts for our publishing program.

Library and Archives Canada Cataloguing in Publication

Boileau, John
     Samuel Cunard : Nova Scotia's master of the North Atlantic / John Boileau.

 Includes bibliographical references and index.
ISBN-13: 978-0-88780-712-1
ISBN-10: 0-88780-712-7

    1. Cunard, Samuel, Sir, 1787-1865. 2. Cunard Steamship Company--History.
3. Merchant mariners--Canada--Biography. I. Title.

HE569.C8B65 2006   387.5092   C2006-903295-5

Formac Publishing Company Limited
5502 Atlantic Street
Halifax, Nova Scotia B3H 1G4
www.formac.ca

Printed and bound in Canada

The Canada Council | Le Conseil des Arts
for the Arts | du Canada

NOVA SCOTIA
Tourism, Culture and Heritage

CONTENTS

PREFACE

The idea for this book came up one day during a casual conversation with Elizabeth Eve, who had worked with me on my two previous books for Formac. We were chatting about various subjects that would make great Nova Scotia stories, and eventually our discussion turned to Samuel Cunard. What follows is the result of that fortuitous meeting. It is the story of a remarkable Nova Scotia entrepreneur — arguably our greatest — who used the ideas and inventions of others to revolutionize transportation and communication.

Steamships did not sweep sailing ships from the world's oceans overnight; the shift took over 50 years. It was a peaceful revolution that began in Sam Cunard's lifetime, was given a major push by him and continued after his death. Cunard deserves a great deal of credit for his foresight and perseverance in expanding the Age of Steam to the North Atlantic, transforming many aspects of the Victorian era. Cunard's steamships were not the first to cross the Atlantic, but they were the most regular and carried the first large mail contract. More importantly, they did not sink. Yet, despite Cunard's triumphs, his achievements are largely unrecognized in his native land. I hope this book contributes, at least in some small way, to changing that view.

In almost all non-fiction writing, the research of others is key, and this book is no different. I have drawn upon the work of several authors, as well as the resources of a number of institutions, to research, write and illustrate it. The Maritime Museum of the Atlantic in Halifax contains an amazing treasure trove of Cunard memorabilia and acknowledges his contribution to the shipping industry in its permanent exhibits. I would like to thank Dan Conlin, Curator, and especially Lynn Marie Richard, the Museum's Registrar, who took time out from her busy daily schedule to offer cheerful assistance in locating numerous Cunard artifacts for me, many tucked away in obscure nooks and crannies.

At the Nova Scotia Archives and Records Management, Reference Archivist Philip Hartling was able to pinpoint exactly the illustrations I needed, while John Price undertook essential visuals research for me at the Library and Archives Canada in Ottawa. I must also thank Jeanne Howell and Michaela Brister at the Cambridge Military Library in Halifax.

At Formac, I would like to thank publisher Jim Lorimer for agreeing to publish this book, and former senior editor Elizabeth Eve (now working with the Canada Council in Ottawa, where I wish her the best of luck) for her support. Thanks are also due to production editor Pam Lutz, graphic designers Marilee MacKay and Meghan Collins, production coordinator Hannah Colville and editorial assistant Erinna Gilkison.

One final note: Throughout the book I have used imperial rather than metric measurements, in keeping with the system used in Cunard's era. Somehow, after all this time, describing a ship as 160 feet long sounds better than stating its length as 48.768 metres.

— *JBB*
August 31, 2006
175th anniversary of the arrival of
Royal William *at Halifax.*

INTRODUCTION — A PARADIGM SHIFT

Until the early part of the nineteenth century, the world was a much bigger place and the pace of life much slower. The speed and the means of transportation and communication had not changed appreciably for thousands of years. Moving people and materials about on land had been governed by the speed of the horse since man first domesticated this fleet, four-footed mammal sometime in prehistory, creating an enduring and endearing partnership. On water, the power of the wind had been the deciding factor in the speed of boats and ships since the development of the sail, a brilliant innovation traceable back almost to the beginning of recorded history.

For centuries, the speed of communication was directly linked to the speed of transportation. Apart from individual travel — and limited, short-range methods such as carrier pigeons or signalling by drums, flags, fires, smoke, semaphore, mirrors and other means — the only way to send a communication over any distance was to dispatch a written document by some form of land or water transport. Then, in the early part of the nineteenth century, simultaneous developments in Britain, Europe and North America ushered in the age of steam transportation. The speed of travel, and thus the speed of communication on land and sea, began to increase dramatically. When the steam engine, originally built as a stationary labour-saving device, was linked to a mechanism capable of motion on special "roads" (i.e., rails), and was then applied to ocean going vessels, the first great revolution in transportation and communication occurred, resulting in locomotives and steamships.

Top: Samuel Cunard ca 1840; Above: Early nineteenth-century view of the northern suburbs of Halifax, where Abraham Cunard settled, from Fort Needham.

Samuel Cunard, born in 1787 in Halifax, the capital of the small British colony of Nova Scotia, became a businessman who took advantage of the sailing ship/steam engine combination and became a key player in revolutionizing the shipping industry. He founded the first regular transatlantic steamship line in 1840 when his flagship *Britannia* arrived in Halifax from Liverpool on her maiden 12½-day crossing.

Cunard's genius led to a major paradigm shift: the first use of regularized transportation and communication by steamship service with advertised and standardized sailings, the nautical equivalent of a railroad timetable.

Artist's interpretation of Samuel Cunard standing on the Dartmouth side of Halifax Harbour, while one of his steamboats sails by behind him.

Cunard, who referred to his scheme as an "ocean railway," established the British and North American Royal Mail Steam Packet Company — usually shortened to the Cunard Line. For a decade, steam transport on the North Atlantic was virtually the sole domain of the Cunard Line. Even when competition arose, Cunard's ships remained pre-eminent for many years.

Samuel Cunard's ideas did not occur in a vacuum. Events entirely outside his control led to the development of the steamship, an invention that, at least initially, most people saw as having little potential. Similarly, the replacement of wooden-hulled ships by iron (and later steel) hulls, and the shift from paddlewheels to screw propellers, were not his ideas, but he made use of them.

Cunard grew up and began his business career in Halifax, one of the world's largest natural harbours, where ships and shipping were an important and transforming facet of the city's economic existence during the nineteenth century. During this time Halifax grew from a small and raucous imperial outpost on the fringes of the Empire to a respectable Victorian town. A large part of the town's wealth was traditionally generated by conflict. When Britain was at war, the merchants, tradesmen and farmers of Halifax prospered by supplying provisions and goods to the Royal Navy and the British Army. During periods of peace, the town's economy tended to suffer. Although Britain was involved in a war somewhere in the world throughout most of the nineteenth century, some of these conflicts were either too small or too remote to influence Halifax's economy.

As Halifax expanded and prospered, a new generation of young, native Nova Scotian entrepreneurs emerged, alert to any opportunity to increase their capital. They began to dominate the local business scene, replacing an older generation of merchants largely financed from abroad. Sam Cunard was one of these young men, and his firm of S. Cunard & Company flourished.

Even after his death in 1865 and well into the twentieth century, Cunard descendants continued to act as directors of the company he founded. Eventually, however, the Cunard family was no longer represented on the company's board. Amalgamations with other steamship lines followed and a new type of service — the cruise ship — came into being, one not specifically dedicated to getting passengers or goods to their destination quickly. The era of the cruise ship ushered in new standards of luxury, ones which the Cunarders readily accepted, then made their own.

The worldwide revolution in transportation and communication that Samuel Cunard started in 1840 continues to this day. The ideas and the legacy of the little man from Halifax who became one of the greatest entrepreneurs of his time have come a long, long way.

1 Religion & Revolution

The story of Samuel Cunard's long journey to success has its roots in two of history's most decisive and divisive recurring patterns — religion and revolution. In the seventeenth century, the Kunders were peace-loving Quakers living in Westphalia, a region in the northwest of what became, almost 200 years later, a united Germany. Thones Kunders, Samuel's great-great-grandfather, was a prosperous dyer and weaver in the medieval city of Crefeld, on the left bank of the Lower Rhine near the Dutch border.

The 1600s were a time of ruthless religious persecution in Europe, the legacy of the Reformation and establishment of Protestantism begun by Martin Luther in 1517. It is believed that the Kunders immigrated to Germany from either Wales or Worcestershire, an English county on the Welsh border, because of religious intolerance in Britain as the Reformation started by Henry VIII took hold there.

In Crefeld, the Kunders did not find the religious freedom they sought and moved again. In July 1683, Thones, his wife Ellen, and their three sons crossed the Atlantic, a journey that took several weeks in *Concord*, a typical creaking and leaking sailing ship of the time. Tossed about as the days dragged by, they could not have imagined the paradigm shift that would be wrought by their descendant in the transatlantic passage in a little over 150 years.

The Kunders and twelve other families — the beginning of German immigration to America — sailed to the Quaker colony of Pennsylvania, founded just two years earlier on lands granted by Charles II to William Penn in payment of a debt. The family settled in Germantown (later a part of Philadelphia), on fertile land near the Delaware River and took up farming. They also engaged in

Above: William Penn, the founder of Pennsylvania, is portrayed in this painting by Thomas Birch (1779–1851); Right: Concord, the ship in which Thomas Kunders and his family crossed the Atlantic Ocean in 1683, as pictured on this 1983 American postage stamp.

textile dying. Their new life on the untamed frontier was a stark contrast to their comfortable existence in Crefeld.

Through hard work the Kunders built up a modest but prosperous farm. Another son and three daughters were added to the family. Legend has it that Thones's prosperity was considerably augmented by an outside source. The many variations on the tale have one thing in common: the discovery of a substantial cache of gold coins, found on the Kunders farm sometime around 1718. Although its source was never ascertained, buried pirate treasure was suspected. If the story is true, it marks the first instance of what later became known as the famous "Cunard luck." Shortly afterwards, perhaps due to his newfound wealth, but with amazing prescience, Thones bought a small coastal vessel in the City of Brotherly Love and started what became a sizeable and profitable shipping fleet.

Over the years, through mispronunciation or misspelling, the family name became Cunrads, then Conrad and, finally, Cunard. Thones's ships followed the lucrative transatlantic trade triangle: America to England, England to the West Indies, the West Indies to Philadelphia, carrying rum, molasses, sugar, fish, tea, coffee, spices and other commodities. When Thones died in 1729, he left a considerable estate to be divided among his seven children, including the successful shipping business. By the time of the American Revolution in 1775, the company was run by Thones's grandson and then his son Abraham. Abraham became the father of Samuel.

The rebellion by the inhabitants of the Thirteen Colonies split families apart and made foes of friends. Not everyone agreed with the rebels' goal of breaking away from the mother country and thousands remained loyal to the British Crown. When the revolution ended in success for the rebels, Abraham Cunard and about 50,000 other Loyalists fled to the British colonies to the north. Two-thirds of them went to Nova Scotia, which at the time included present-day New Brunswick.

In the spring of 1783, exactly 100 years after religious persecution drove the Cunard ancestors to America, revolutionary fervour forced their descendants from America.

Abraham sailed from the Loyalist stronghold of New York in convoy with some 20 other ships. Among the 200 displaced Loyalists aboard his vessel was the family of Thomas Murphy from Charleston, South Carolina, who had emigrated from Ireland only 10 years earlier. The two families knew each other, as the South Carolinian had built ships for the Cunard firm before the revolution. During the voyage, the quiet, 27-year-old Abraham Cunard met the spirited, 25-year-old Margaret Murphy, a girl taller than he. Before their ship reached its destination, they were in love.

The Loyalists received large tracts of land from the British government, as well as clothing, provisions, lumber and tools to help them get established and build their new homes. Thomas Murphy chose land near the settlement of Rawdon, in the hills north of Halifax, where several soldiers who had fought under Lord Rawdon in South Carolina had recently established themselves. In common with many Southerners, Murphy brought his slaves with him to cut down the forests and work the resulting cleared fields. Abraham settled in Halifax.

The American Revolution had quickly changed Halifax from a sleepy little outpost — founded in 1749 as a bulwark against the mighty French fortress of Louisburg on Cape Breton Island — to a bustling seaport for prosecuting the war against the rebellious Thirteen Colonies. It quickly became the biggest and most important military and naval base in British North America. British infantry soldiers occupied barracks on the lower slopes of the Citadel, the wooden fortress that topped the hill overlooking the busy harbour and the various blockhouses protecting the landward approaches to the town.

Other red-coated regiments spilled out into a crowded tented encampment on Camp Hill, across the marshy Commons from Citadel Hill. In Halifax's large harbour, ice-free in all but the coldest winters, warships of the Royal Navy rested at anchor, protected by the many Royal Artillery shore batteries that guarded its entrance. Vessels underwent repairs in the extensive dockyard, while still others were fitted out with ammunition, provisions and

An idealized depiction of the arrival of Loyalists on the rocky shores of Nova Scotia, painted by Canadian-born artist Henry Sandham (1842–1910).

naval stores from its warehouses before venturing forth to teach the defiant American colonists a lesson. In the end, it was the British who learned the lesson.

The arrival of hundreds of Loyalists only added to the overcrowding in the town. Permanent housing was in short supply and most of the Loyalists were put up in tents and in ships' deckhouses on vacant lots along Halifax's streets. Conditions were deplorable. There was no sewage system and backyard privies were filled to overflowing, when their foul mess ran downhill. Most of it didn't make it to the harbour, but collected in odiferous puddles or made its way into the town pumps. When outhouses were emptied, their contents were carried to the harbour in wheelbarrows or handcarts and dumped into the water. Nightly slops were emptied directly into the gutters, adding to the filth already there. Disease lurked at every street corner.

With so many civilian and military mouths to feed, food was scarce, especially fresh food. For most of the year, the staple was salt meat or salt fish, a few potatoes and bread, a diet that frequently led to scurvy, caused by a lack of vitamin C. Prices of almost everything rose. The only thing in plentiful supply was cheap West Indian rum, consumed in vast quantities by civilians, soldiers and sailors alike. Drunkenness and sickness were rampant. Both of these conditions reached deep into the Cunard family and caused irreparable harm.

For those who wanted to grow their own food, the soil on the rockbound coast of the colony was extremely poor. Any farming was marginal at best. For the Loyalists, it was a very different standard of living from the Thirteen Colonies and many of them wondered if their loyalty to the Crown was worth it. They soon began to call Nova Scotia by a new name: Nova Scarcity.

A number of Loyalists decided they weren't prepared to face the hardships of living in the colony and sailed to Britain. For those who stayed, their existence continued to be defined by meager government handouts. In one area, however, the Crown was fairly generous: land. Every Loyalist was entitled to a grant. For his grant, Abraham

Cunard wisely chose a shore lot, a narrow 10-acre strip running downhill to the waterfront. It was on land in the north end of Halifax, in a German section known as Dutchtown, between the built up area and the naval dockyard.

Abraham, a carpenter, designed and built a small, unpainted, two-storey house of squared timber near the top of the hill, just north of what is now Proctor Street, behind what eventually became 257 Brunswick Street. His carpentry skills and his knowledge of ships also got him a job, a lucky turn in the cyclical, conflict dependent Halifax economy. He was hired by the Royal Engineers to work in the government lumberyard (on the site of today's Westin Hotel), where masts, spars and squared timber were trimmed to size for use by the navy and army. With a house and steady employment, Quaker Abraham married Catholic Margaret and moved her into their new home. They became Anglicans, perhaps as a religious compromise or possibly because of the benefits that could accrue to members of the only denomination officially sanctioned by the state.

Margaret bore Abraham seven sons and two daughters. Their first child, Mary, was born in 1784. Their second child and first son, born on November 21, 1787, was christened Samuel, but was usually known by everyone as Sam. Seven more followed: William, Susan, Edward, Joseph (who became the second most famous Cunard), John, Thomas and Henry. From the beginning, the family had to contend with Margaret's alcoholism, which they tried unsuccessfully to keep secret. In later years, neighbours told stories of finding Margaret passed out on the city's streets from the effects of drink, while her children had no shoes to wear.

This private struggle played out behind the public drama of Halifax's fortunes, which rose and fell with war and peace. The end of the Revolutionary War hit Halifax with a double whammy: Britain refused to let Nova Scotia trade with the Americans and most of the Royal Navy ships and British Army regiments left the town. A postwar depression resulted.

Although many of the Loyalists (some of whom were not wealthy to begin with) were reduced to dire circum-

Above: Government House in Halifax, built as the official residence of the Lieutenant-Governor during Wentworth's time as portrayed by artist J. E. Woolford; Right: Sir John Wentworth.

stances, their previous status in American society carried over to Halifax's colonial social order. A new resident living in a rough hewn, earthen floor, one-room log cabin might find himself fully accepted as a member of the town's established upper class, mixing and mingling with Lieutenant-Governor John Parr (or later John Wentworth, a fellow Loyalist), senior colonial staff, army and naval officers, the bishop and the mercantile elite.

Many a Loyalist would dress in whatever pre-war finery they had managed to salvage and make their way from a tiny house along muddy lanes to the governor's residence, for balls and banquets, receptions and repasts. It was at such events that important contacts were made, often resulting in jobs, appointments and contracts for the Loyalists.

When Sam was only five years old, an event occurred that made a deep impression and even affected his future business ventures. Since 1785 a group of Loyalist whalers — Quakers originally from Nantucket — operated from the Dartmouth side of Halifax Harbour. Their 27 whalers sailed the South Atlantic on multi-year cruises in search of their valuable quarry, which they brought back to two whale-oil factories in Dartmouth. Besides employing sailors and factory workers, a support industry grew up in the area to service the fleet. People prospered.

An early nineteenth-century view of Milford Haven in Wales.

In 1792 an imperial and imperious government ordered the fleet to Milford Haven in Wales, to help support the British whaling industry and home trade. Halifax merchants were stunned and objected to the government's autocratic action, but to no avail. Abraham Cunard joined their protest and for years afterwards referred to the sad "day they took the whalemen." Sam remembered the day in August when the whaling fleet departed and later vowed he would someday do something about it.

Two years after the whaling fleet departed, Halifax's citizens were abuzz with the notion that their town had finally achieved high standing in the Empire. Prince Edward, Duke of Kent, soldier-son of mad King George III, arrived as Commander-in-Chief for Nova Scotia in 1794, after tours at Gibraltar and Quebec. He brought his mistress, the beautiful, enigmatic Madame Julie de St. Laurent, whom he set up in Prince's Lodge, a secluded love nest along the wooded shores of Bedford Basin. Halifax society was heady with the thought of a royal prince in their midst. Sam was swept along in the enthusiasm for Edward and the sight of the tall soldier striding the town's streets, resplendent in full-dress uniform, likely influenced his later decision to join one of Halifax's elite militia regiments.

During his time in Halifax, the Duke made several important improvements to the town's defences (which contributed about £100,000 pounds to Halifax's economy, an enormous amount for the time). He ordered the Old Town Clock built to keep the garrison and Haligonians on time (ironically, it arrived late from England, after Edward departed). He also established a semaphore telegraph system for sending information across the colony, the first of its kind in North America.

Edward was a rigid martinet who ordered floggings for the pettiest of offences, and a spendthrift, already over £20,000 in debt when he arrived in Halifax. Only six years later, Edward returned to England, where, under orders to produce an heir for the throne (his older brother, who ruled as William IV, was childless), he put aside Julie after 27 years together and married German Princess Victoire of Saxe-Coburg-Saalfield. In 1819, just eight months before he died, he did his royal duty and fathered the future Queen Victoria.

When prosperity started to return to Halifax in 1793, at the beginning of Britain's long war against Revolutionary

France, many of the struggling Loyalists grew rich on army and navy contracts with the expansion of military and naval facilities in Halifax. If any such financial attractions were offered to Abraham, he didn't accept them. He worked diligently at his job and rose to the position of foreman carpenter. In 1799 the Duke of Kent, Commander-in-Chief for Nova Scotia, appointed Abraham master carpenter to the Contingent Department of the Royal Engineers. Abraham supplemented his income by designing and building houses, for which he hired men to assist him. He may have needed the extra income because of his large, growing family, or to cover the money spent by Margaret on rum. Perhaps work was his way of dealing with her alcoholism.

Abraham eventually replaced his original house with a larger one on the same lot and bought another piece of property on Brunswick Street, initially as a pasture for the family cow. One of young Sam's chores was to take the cow to and from the pasture. Abraham also expanded his waterfront property by adding two more lots, for which he paid £800, a considerable sum at the time.

Sam was educated at home until he was eight, a normal practice at the time, and then he attended the Halifax Grammar School, an opportunity not many children shared as it was the only day school in the town for boys, public or private. His education included the typical subjects of the day: English, French, Latin and Greek; writing, mathematics, astronomy, natural philosophy and elocution. Despite being a bright student who was particularly good at figures, Sam saw little use for Latin, Greek and elocution. His limited education revealed itself throughout his life; his spelling and grammar were inconsistent and he was always reluctant to speak in public. In later years, he remarked, "a plain English education answers the purpose" of anyone "intended for business." And at an early age, Sam Cunard decided he was clearly intended for business, believing that an ambitious young man should chose the life of a merchant over a government position, which "frequently leads to old age with a small pittance but little removed from poverty."

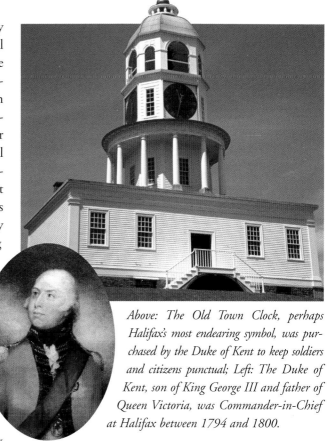

Above: The Old Town Clock, perhaps Halifax's most endearing symbol, was purchased by the Duke of Kent to keep soldiers and citizens punctual; Left: The Duke of Kent, son of King George III and father of Queen Victoria, was Commander-in-Chief at Halifax between 1794 and 1800.

Sam recognized the potential pitfalls of a career in business. "'Tis true that the merchant does not always succeed," he observed in later life, "— but with patient industry he generally does — there is one thing certain that no one succeeds without application and close attention to the business he is intended for." Stories abound about Sam's early industriousness and interest in business. One journalist later noted, "It is a pity more lads do not follow his example, they might be a credit to their families."

Sam may have had no choice in the matter. The effect his mother's alcoholism had on his desire to be successful is not known, but it likely influenced his efforts to bring extra cash into the family. Supposedly, while driving the cow to and from pasture, he knit a heelless sock (other versions have his mother knitting it for him) and added a drawstring to make a moneybag, similar to the leather pouches he saw tucked into

The British captured the French frigate La Tribune *in 1796 and recommissioned her into the royal Navy as* HMS Tribune. *A year later she was wrecked in Halifax's harbour.*

the belts of Halifax's prosperous merchants as they walked along the town's grimy streets. He needed the moneybag for he soon learned that industriousness resulted in income.

In an era of limited transportation and communication — sectors of society he would revolutionize as an adult — Sam ran errands and delivered letters. When his mother sent him to buy vegetables at the Merkel farm on the edge of town, he delivered produce to other customers. He picked dandelion greens on the Commons in the spring (joining throngs of others who savoured the fresh delicacy after the long winter) and sold them in the market. With his earnings, he made his way to the wharves where traders auctioned their cargoes, to bid on small broken lots of tea, coffee and spices. When he was successful, he repackaged his purchases and then peddled them door-to-door to the good matrons of Halifax. At fourteen, he bought his first broadcloth suit with his own money. Sam Cunard was undoubtedly destined for business.

As the oldest boy, his mother's alcoholism forced Sam to assume responsibilities at an early age. Her illness also affected his personal characteristics, and was partially responsible for making him the quiet, inward-looking adult he became. His rigid self-discipline over his emotions, his reticence to reveal his character in public and his close reliance on family for mutual support, can all be traced back to his childhood experience of growing up with an alcoholic parent. Later in life he observed, "I have never known an industrious sober man who has not succeeded," undoubtedly an indirect reference to his mother's disease.

The mere fact of living in an important seaport, where the continuous comings and goings of squat, square-rigged merchantmen, Royal Mail packets, sleek fishing schooners, slow coasters, jaunty privateers, huge two-and three-decker men-of-war and fast frigates, also influenced Sam and provided him with a living panorama at his window. Moreover, for an adventurous boy, there was the thrill of wandering through the docks, catching first-hand the striking sights, sounds and smells of sailors and ships from around the world. Sea-going vessels became his great love.

Shipwrecks were a frequent occurrence along Nova Scotia's fog-sheathed and rock-bound coast. One particular incident that happened two days after Sam's 10th birthday in 1797, drove home the dangerous side of shipping. Through a piloting error, the Royal Navy frigate *Tribune* ran aground on Thrumcap Shoals, off McNab's Island at the harbour's mouth. Rescue boats tried to reach the ship, but huge breakers and high winds forced them back. By evening, the tide lifted a now severely damaged *Tribune* off the rocks and sent her across the harbour mouth only to ground again, 30 feet off the entrance to Herring Cove. She began to fill. In the pounding surf nothing could be done to save those on board. Their screams were heard throughout the night. All but 12 of her 248 crew members drowned. Over the next few days, battered bodies washed up along the shore, to be carted off for a mass burial. Such a vivid demonstration of the power of the sea, and of the dangers of uncharted waters and lack of lighthouses, made a lasting impression on Sam. His memories of that fateful day had a profound influence on the character of the steamship line that he founded years later.

2 CUNARD & COMPANY

Samuel Cunard, in the 1850s.

Like his father, Sam Cunard was of less than average height. Alert and intelligent, he had keen brown eyes, a high brow, a firm mouth set in narrow jaws and "happy manners." His small frame belied his great energy and his strength — physical as well as mental. In his youth, he could stay up and dance until the early hours of the morning and still be wide-awake and fresh for the next day's activities. His well-known youthful sociability did not lessen his determination, single-mindedness and strength of character, which one friend described as his ability to "make both events and people bend to his will."

Sam believed success was achieved only through diligent application and careful attention to the business at hand. He possessed the useful knack of being able to choose subordinates who were similarly inclined: hard-working, loyal men of superior talent whom he inspired to exert themselves as he did. His workers considered him "just, but not generous." Those who knew him spoke of his "brisk step, quick and ready movements, and his air of 'push'." Sam's greatest strength was his resolve to succeed as a businessman, a goal he achieved far beyond what he, or anyone else from Halifax, ever imagined was possible.

Sam left the Halifax Grammar School in 1804, when he was 17, having received more formal education than most children from his social class at the time. He got a job as a clerk at the Royal Engineers' lumberyard, undoubtedly arranged by his father, where he worked for a year at a salary of seven shillings and sixpence a day, plus £20 a year lodging allowance. He drafted and copied designs, and checked specifications of masts, spars and timber. Abraham then got him a position in the office of a ship-broker in Boston, America's largest port and a town the British Army had evacuated for Halifax less than 30 years earlier. Sam spent three years as a clerk in the Massachusetts town, from 1805 to 1808, copying out ships' manifests, recording which merchants' cargoes came and went on which ships, advertising sailings and learning everything he could about shipping and international trade. Boston was a good place to do this as it grew in importance and became a major port. Hundreds of ships sailed to and from the far corners of the world in search of goods and markets. It was not the last time Boston would figure prominently in Sam's life. He was well treated there and, in due course, he would repay the kindness many times over.

While Sam was in Boston, Abraham continued to expand his business. The foresight in his decision to choose a water-front lot paid handsome dividends and he established Cunard's Wharf at the foot of his property, a landing stage

that soon became one of the harbour's busiest. The prosperity that returned to Halifax when the war against Revolutionary France began in 1793 took a giant leap upward with the beginning of the Peninsular War against Napoleon in 1808. Halifax merchants became richer than ever. One of the most prosperous was shrewd Enos Collins, whose three ships ran the French blockade to supply British troops besieged at Cadiz in Spain. It was time for the Cunards to expand again.

When 21-year-old Sam returned from Boston, he was fired with entrepreneurial zeal. His experience in the ship-broker's office had showed him the money that could be made in the shipping business. He convinced his father to found a shipping firm: A. Cunard & Son. They ordered their first ship, the small schooner *Margaret*, from Tom Murphy, *Margaret's* brother, who had settled on Prince Edward Island and established a shipyard there.

Left: Sextant, used to determine longitude; Below: View of the Naval Yard, Halifax, 1796, with the Commissioner's house in the centre.

Their decision began to pay dividends almost immediately, as the little coaster carried trade goods from Halifax to nearby ports. At about the same time, Sam became a landowner. He purchased 5,000 acres in the sparsely settled northeastern part of the colony, a purely speculative venture against the day he might make a profit from rents, timber or minerals. His business interests were already beginning to branch out in different directions; many more would follow.

Besides making money by supplying goods and provisions to the army and navy, many Halifax merchants invested in privateers, a form of government-licenced piracy. By obtaining a letter of marque, issued by the governor on behalf of the Crown, civilian ships, outfitted with a few cannons and other warlike stores, were allowed to prey on the enemy's merchant shipping. Once seized vessels, known as prizes, were adjudicated by the Court of Vice-Admiralty in Halifax as a valid capture, they were sold at auction along with their cargoes. The Cunard's second ship, *Nancy*, was such a prize, a sloop captured from the French off the island of St. Pierre. *Nancy*, under command of one of Sam's younger brothers, William, went further afield than *Margaret*. Will carried flour and sugar to the Miramichi region of New Brunswick, and brought back dried fish for trade with the West Indies.

Just as A. Cunard & Son was beginning to enjoy some success, the family received bad news. Mary, Abraham and Margaret's first child, had died during an epidemic of yellow fever in Barbados, along with her husband, Captain John Parr of the Royal Navy, and their baby daughter. When this news reached her parents in the spring of 1811, it was a blow from which they never recovered. Abraham was not a robust man and his health deteriorated, while Margaret's abuse of alcohol, which had been a serious and embarrassing problem for years, got worse. Sam took more control of the business from his father.

Halifax's fortunes rose yet again, as the war against France took on a local aspect when the little North American sideshow to the main European event began in 1812. The War of 1812 brought the Royal Navy and British Army back to Halifax in numbers that had not

President James Madison declared war on Britain on June 18, 1812, starting the War of 1812.

been seen since the American Revolution. They were there to prosecute a war against America for the second time in less than 30 years. Although President James Madison had declared war on Great Britain, the people of New England wanted no part of "Mr. Madison's War." Similarly, the residents of the Maritimes, long linked to New England by ties of family and trade, were not inclined to fight against their neighbour.

A truce between the two regions quickly followed, so that trade could be carried on to their mutual benefit. With safe conduct passes issued by their respective local governments, ships of both countries continued their lucrative business. In fact, if it had not been for American goods supplied to the British and vice versa, the British could not have prosecuted the war against the United States — and vice versa.

By July 6, 1812 — within a week of Madison's declara-

An artistic portrayal of tavern fighting.

Luck, which rapidly became known as a Cunard characteristic, also played its part in the company's fortunes. In early 1814, *Margaret,* carrying a valuable cargo of sugar, molasses and rum, was captured by an American privateer on a return journey from the West Indies island of Martinique. The ship was then recaptured and brought to Halifax. In accordance with the complex, rigid rules governing such recaptures, on payment of one-eighth of the value of her cargo, Judge Alexander Croke of the Court of Vice-Admiralty returned her to the Cunards, saving them from a potential disaster.

The Cunards' West Indian trade continued to grow, and they imported spirits, molasses, brown sugar and coffee from the islands, as well as from the Dutch colonies of Demerara and Surinam on the nearby South American coast. Based on Sam's Boston experience, the company also acted as agents for ships owned by others.

As the War of 1812 progressed, Abraham turned more and more of the business over to Sam. While Abraham stayed in the office looking after the employees and the books, Sam was up at dawn and down at the bustling waterfront, where he bought and sold cargoes, supervised the loading and unloading of ships and made deals. It was a rare individual who outdid Sam Cunard in any transaction; he generally got the best of any bargain.

With the growth in his business, Sam also participated in other aspects of Halifax life. He joined a local militia unit, the 2nd Battalion, Halifax Regiment, nicknamed the "Scarlet Runners" after their colourful full-dress uniforms. Eventually, he became one of the battalion's captains. In 1809, the year after his return from Boston, Sam had been chosen by secret ballot to join the exclusive Sun Fire Company. In the days before publicly funded fire protection services, volunteer fire companies provided firefighting services in towns and cities. At a time when most structures were built of wood, these organizations were often all that prevented entire towns from going up in flames when a fire broke out. Besides public-spiritedness, there was another good reason to belong to the Sun Fire

tion of war — A. Cunard & Son received one of the first permits for such trade from Lieutenant-Governor Sir John Sherbrooke. It was a significant boost to the firm's growth. Once again, world events had conspired to have a direct and profound influence upon Sam's business dealings.

The Cunards acquired their third vessel in 1813, a captured square-rigger, *White Oak*, bought at prize auction. In July, the Cunards announced that this ship would sail to London in the first available convoy under Royal Navy escort and had "good accommodation for passengers," their first foray into the passenger trade. The success of *White Oak*'s crossing enabled the Cunards to buy another ship, which was sent to the West Indies loaded with a cargo of dried fish and returned with molasses and sugar.

The War of 1812 turned Halifax into a boomtown. With the arrival of thousands of sailors and soldiers, the population doubled and drove prices up. Merchants and tradesmen reaped fantastic profits supplying and servicing the navy and army. A. Cunard & Son was doing better than either Abraham or Sam had thought possible. Further expansion saw the company selling timber from its Miramichi holdings to the Halifax military lumberyard and abroad, usually in Britain. This activity was overseen by Joe, a flamboyant younger brother.

The first fire wagon ever used in Halifax, dating from the 1750s, which saw service through Cunard's time in the Sun Fire Company.

Company. Many of its members came from the town's mercantile elite, a source of valuable contacts for an enterprising young man intent on scaling business — as well as fire fighting — ladders. Sam rose in this organization as well; he became its president in 1821. An appointment as one of the town's fire wardens followed. He was responsible for directing fire companies as they fought fires and deciding which buildings would be demolished as a last resort to prevent the spread of a fire.

In the summer of 1814, 26-year-old Sam became engaged to the 19-year-old Susan Duffus, the attractive oldest daughter of William Duffus, a wealthy Halifax dry goods merchant and tailor, and his wife, Susannah. Sam and Susan's half brother, James, now a Royal Navy lieutenant, had been students together at the Halifax Grammar School.

William Duffus, who had come to Halifax on a visit from Scotland as a young man, decided to stay and set up a business importing fine cloth from Britain. Within a few years, he was getting rich supervising a stable of tailors who turned out custom-made uniforms for the naval and army officers who filled the town during wartime. He also kept a stable of expensive horses. As a boy, Sam had often seen William and Susannah, a noted beauty, riding on the Commons dressed in finery produced in the Duffus tailor shop.

Susan and Sam were married in the drawing room of her parents' imposing residence on Saturday, February 4, 1815, by the rector of St. Paul's Church. The newly married couple moved immediately into a four-story house Sam had recently built on Brunswick Street — by now a busy main road — next to his parent's home. The little dwelling originally built by Abraham now housed the servants. The waterfront and Cunard's Wharf were clearly visible from the house and, on Monday morning, Sam was back at work.

Both William and Susannah Duffus regarded Sam as an eminently suitable match for their daughter. Along with other businessmen, William had been following Sam's career and frequently discussed it with other merchants. They agreed he was destined for even greater triumphs.

A month after the wedding, word arrived in Halifax of the signing of the Treaty of Ghent in the Belgian city on

Christmas Eve, 1814, ending the War of 1812. Almost three years of war with the United States had resulted in little change. Both sides went back to the *status quo ante bellum*. In August, 1815, even more important military news reached Halifax, reporting the Duke of Wellington's great victory over Napoleon Bonaparte at Waterloo in June. For the first time since 1793, apart from the few months respite brought by the Treaty of Amiens in 1802–1803, Britain was not at war.

Even with the end of the war, Sam's business continued to expand. That same summer, the firm purchased two lots in Halifax's northern suburbs at public auction for £1,325, properties no longer needed by the military, where additional wharves and warehouses were built. On the recommendation of Surveyor General Charles Morris, the Cunards received valuable water rights 500 feet out into the harbour, because of "their well known character, for active exertion and enterprise in useful improvements and commercial pursuits."

Sam had also purchased another piece of property that summer, one that had nothing to do with the business. In June, when Susan was three months pregnant with their first son, Edward, Sam bought land at Pleasant Valley, near Rawdon, where his mother's parents had settled after coming from the United States. He built a story-and-a-half house there, with a covered verandah along its front. Sam sent his mother to live in the house, near her relatives, although perhaps banished would be a better term. Abraham, apparently willingly, stayed in Halifax and continued to work. The reason for Sam's actions can be surmised. Neighbours believed he wanted to get Margaret out of town and away from the demon rum. Combined with the impending arrival of his firstborn, the supervision of his two youngest brothers still at home, and general social embarrassment, Sam had good reason to distance himself from his mother's drinking.

In the fall of 1815, Sam expanded the company's shipping activities yet again. He made the first of many trips to Britain and secured what was to be the first of his many Royal Mail contracts from the British govern-

View across the Halifax Commons towards the Citadel, where Sam often saw his future parents-in-law riding.

A view of St. Paul's Church, overlooking Halifax's Grand Parade, ca 1819. Sam and his wife, Susan, were married by the Church's rector in 1815 in her parents' home.

ment. At the time, mail was carried to Halifax on the Falmouth packets, 200-ton brigs named after their British port of departure. The service had started in 1755 and, although it was supposed to be regularized with packets sailing on the first Thursday of every month, the little ships didn't sail until they had enough passengers to make the voyage profitable. Depending on the prevailing westerly winds, the journey normally took between four to eight weeks, but could take as long as 12 weeks in rough weather. From Halifax, the mail was sent to other British colonies on the first available vessel, which might not be for several weeks, an uncertain prac-

tice at best. Sam's contract replaced this system and called for his ships to carry the mail from Halifax to Boston, St. John's, Newfoundland and, later, Bermuda. He quickly established a reputation for reliability with the British postal authorities, a reputation that would pay handsome dividends in the coming years.

The delivery of mail to Canada (Ontario and Quebec) was even more problematic because of the difficulty of navigating the Gulf of St. Lawrence and the St. Lawrence River. Sam overcame this problem with the establishment of the Overland Express. From Halifax, the mail was carried in letter bags by riders on fast horses 140 miles to

Annapolis Royal, across the Bay of Fundy to Saint John by ship, up the Saint John and Madawaska rivers and Lake Temiscouata by canoe, and then overland by a rough and rocky 36-mile-long portage to the St. Lawrence River. From there, it was carried overland or by ship up the river. During winter, when the Saint John and other waterways froze, the mail bypassed Halifax and went directly to Boston, and then overland to Quebec.

The end of war inevitably meant the return of naval and military forces to Britain — and the return of hard times to Halifax. It took about a year for this shift to happen. Without the wartime requirements of the military for beef, pork and hay, trade declined and jobs disappeared. An invasion of thousands of rodents devoured farmers' crops in 1815 — "The Year of the Mice" — followed by "The Year with No Summer" in 1816, when frosts in June and July caused extensive crop damage. Halifax's economy received yet another blow in 1819 when the Naval Board abruptly moved the headquarters of the North America and West Indies Station to Bermuda from October to May annually, without giving any reason for their decision. With the fleet and its sailors and shore staff gone for half of each year, the result was far less money in the hands of local tradesmen and merchants, as well as tavern owners and prostitutes.

The only things that increased at this time were poverty, hunger and the number of immigrants: British settlers trying to start a new life, black refugees from Chesapeake Bay plantations, discharged British soldiers. Even the wealthy were affected. Without officers to be outfitted in fancy uniforms, William Duffus's business faltered, then failed. Duffus went bankrupt. An attempt to re-establish himself with borrowed money ended when his warehouse burned down. Susannah took in boarders in an effort to earn money, but it proved impractical. In the end, Sam supported them with a pension of £300 a year.

If some of the well off felt the pinch of hard times, those at the bottom of the social pyramid were overwhelmed. Even during the good years, about one quarter of Halifax's population relied on handouts from the Poor Society. The Society in turn depended on donations from the wealthy to help feed, clothe and accommodate their deprived brethren. The Countess of Dalhousie, the wife of Nova Scotia's new lieutenant-governor, George Ramsay, Earl of Dalhousie, was particularly concerned about the plight of the poor. She persuaded the colonial administration (no doubt helped by the fact she was married to its head) to provide funds for poor relief. Dalhousie appointed Sam and merchant Michael Tobin as trustees. For the next four winters, from 1817 to 1821, Cunard and Tobin oversaw kitchens set up on the Grand Parade in the centre of Halifax, which doled out hot soup and bread twice a day to about 500 people, while Susan collected food and clothing for the town's many new immigrants. Sam Cunard was being noticed for more than his business acumen.

A view of the upper end of St. John's Harbour, ca 1800. One of Sam's early contracts was to deliver mail to Newfoundland.

3 WHALES & WILDFIRES

A year after the War of 1812 began, a young Royal Navy officer arrived in Halifax as part of the war effort against the United States. On June 7, 1813, Lieutenant William Edward Parry (1790–1855) sailed into Halifax Harbour in the 74-gun man-of-war *La Hogue* under Captain the Honourable Thomas Bladen Capel. Parry, a friend of Susan's half brother, James, a fellow naval lieutenant, was a regular visitor at the Cunard home and befriended Sam. Their conversations, of which there were many (Parry became ill and spent several months recovering in Halifax, eventually serving there for four years), frequently turned to the young officer's dream of finding the fabled and elusive Northwest Passage. After Halifax, Parry participated in five Arctic expeditions (1818–27) and commanded the last four. Although he did not find the Northwest Passage, he stands in the first rank of great northern navigators and established a record for reaching furthest north that stood for 50 years. Parry's efforts contributed greatly to the eventual discovery of the Northwest Passage and the North Pole.

Before Parry left Halifax, Sam fulfilled an ambition he and his father had long cherished. With the end of the war, he was searching for new means of making money and revived their old dream of re-establishing the local whaling fleet. Outfitting a whaler for a two-year voyage to the South Atlantic was a costly venture, so instead Sam sent the brig *Rachel* to the Strait of Belle Isle on a summer cruise in 1817. The crew had a poor return for their efforts — only 90 barrels of oil — but it was moot in any case.

Engraving of Sir William Edward Parry, who served in Halifax as a lieutenant.

On her return journey, *Rachel* ran into a fierce storm off the coast of Newfoundland. The whaler, driven ashore, broke apart on the rocks. Fortunately, the crew made it to safety.

Not one to be easily discouraged, the next year Sam asked the government for financial support for a longer cruise to the South Atlantic, maintaining that restoration of the industry would benefit the colony. The government agreed. Sam outfitted the brig *Prince of Waterloo* for an 18-month voyage off Brazil from 1819 to 1821. Although the whaler returned safely to Halifax, oil collected barely paid her costs. Her second voyage the next year, to the Strait of Belle Isle, proved no better than her first.

Sam was not used to failure, and three in a row gave him pause. He still wanted to re-establish the local whaling industry, but realized that he would have to follow the lead recently taken by the New England whalers, the best in the world at the time. They had left the Atlantic fishery for the more profitable Pacific one, a venture requiring three-year cruises, bigger vessels and more money. The government denied the Cunards' latest request for assistance, and Abraham and Sam did not have sufficient capital for such a tremendous outlay. Sam did not want to abandon the whale fishery, but he decided to set the idea aside temporarily, to be resurrected when conditions were more favourable.

Sam and Susan's son Edward, born on the last day of 1815, was followed by Mary, born in 1817, Susan (who died in infancy) in 1819, and Margaret Ann (Margaret) in 1820. No longer trying to run a boarding house, Susannah, Susan's mother, spent much of her time looking after her grandchildren to her — and their — great delight.

In 1820 Abraham retired and joined his wife Margaret, at the Rawdon country house. Two of their sons, Will and Henry, also moved to Rawdon to help run the farm, a task that seemed too much for Abraham. Abraham and Margaret spent only a year and a half together in retirement. Margaret died in December 1821. Abraham followed her in January 1824. They lie beside each other in the little rural cemetery of St. Paul's Church in Rawdon.

When Abraham moved to the country, Sam became the head of the firm and on May 1, 1824, a few months after his father's death, he changed its name to S. Cunard & Company. The company's headquarters were now in a newly constructed office and warehouse on Upper Water Street, an imposing four-story structure built of ironstone from nearby Purcell's Cove. The building, with a 110-foot frontage, had a large arched passageway in the middle that provided secure access to the wharf.

The oldest sons, Sam, Will and Joe, as trustees of Abraham's estate, traded some of the businesses between themselves over the next couple of years. Eventually a loose partnership emerged between Sam and his brothers Joe and Edward (Will had died in a shipwreck). Abraham's three younger sons, John, Tom and Henry, were not part of the company. Joe, only 22, later assisted by Henry (freed from duties at the Rawdon country place), moved to the Miramichi River region of northeastern New Brunswick the same year that his father retired to the country. He established Joseph Cunard & Company, with Sam as a partner, to oversee the family's forest

Left: Watercolour of Lower Water Street, Halifax, 1823, by Charles Chichester; Above: The brass plaque that was displayed on the offices and warehouse of S. Cunard & Co., now part of the Maritime Museum of the Atlantic's extensive Samuel Cunard collection.

holdings, large tracts of the King's Woods south of the river to which the Cunards had acquired the timber rights.

It was at this point in Sam's career that technological advances were to factor significantly in his business decisions. Although the power of steam had been known for centuries, no practical application was realized until 1698, when English military engineer Thomas Savery developed a steam engine capable of lifting water. Over the next hundred years, others tinkered with and improved his invention, most notably Englishman Thomas Newcomen (1663–1729) and Scotsman James Watt (1736–1819). At the beginning of the nineteenth century, inventors successfully married the steam engine to a boat in Scotland and to a railway carriage in Wales. Two of the great technological landmarks in the progress of civilization occurred almost simultaneously. The world was about to take a giant step forward into the Industrial Age, an advance that changed it forever.

Although several inventors experimented with coupling the power of steam to a ship, many credit American Robert Fulton (1765–1815) with the invention of the steamboat. Discredited would perhaps be a better description, as it appears he copied the ideas and designs of others without acknowledgment — or permission. His later lies, forgeries and dishonesty add substance to this conclusion. Fulton demonstrated his first steamboat in France in 1803, 20 years after *Pyroscaphe*, built by Frenchman Claude de Jouffroy d'Abbans, steamed near Lyons for 15 minutes. In America, inventor John Fitch (1743–98) demonstrated steam-powered craft in 1786, before Fulton even went to France. When Fulton returned to America, he continued the experiments begun in

Artist's depiction of Fulton's Clermont *steaming up the Hudson River between New York and Albany in 1807; Right: Robert Fulton and his steamboat* Clermont *are shown on this 1965 American postage stamp issued on the bicentennial of his birth.*

France with the 150-foot-long ship *Steamboat*, driven by an engine built in Britain and installed in a hull of his design. In August 1807, *Steamboat* steamed up the Hudson River from New York to the state capital at Albany, a distance of 150 miles, at an average speed of five miles an hour. With numerous improvements and a new name — *Clermont* — Fulton's ship went into regular service between New York and Albany, the world's first continuous commercial use of a ship powered by steam — and Fulton's lasting claim to fame.

Early steamboats used paddlewheels for propulsion, either at the sides or the stern. In North America, with its many navigable rivers and lakes, steamboats developed into large, relatively fast, shallow-draft vessels, unsuitable for ocean travel. Undoubtedly influenced by Fulton's success, Montreal brewer John Molson (1763–1836) inaugurated the first steamer passenger service in Canada on the St. Lawrence River. Although shipbuilding was well advanced in Canada at the time, metalworking was not, yet Molson boldly decided that both his ship *and* her engine would be manufactured in Canada. The 85-foot long *Accommodation* was launched on August 9, 1809. She made her first voyage on November 1 from Montreal to Quebec in 36 hours (another 30 hours was spent at anchor during the trip). *Accommodation* was powered by a six-horsepower, coal-fired engine, cast at the Forges St. Maurice. The price for passage was eight dollars downriver and nine dollars upriver, provisions included. The *Quebec Mercury*, commenting on the trip, hit on the fundamental superiority of steam over sail: "The great advantage attending a vessel so constructed is, that a passage may be calculated on to a degree of certainty, in point of time; which cannot be the case with any vessel propelled by sails only."

Although *Accommodation* was a failure commercially (much of her time was spent undergoing alterations or repairs), she marks a milestone in the history of steam: the first steamboat in Canada, the first to be built entirely outside of Britain, and the third to enter commercial service anywhere in the world. After several improvements had been incorporated into *Accommodation*, during her second and last season, Molson journeyed to the United States for discussions with Fulton. Fulton convinced Molson to use British-built engines, which he did in his next steamboats.

While cruising in H.M.S. *Niger* on the St. Lawrence River in the summer of 1816, Lieutenant Edward Parry observed "a truly wonderful piece of mechanism" making its way down river at nine knots. It was *Accommodation*'s replacement, *Swiftsure*, launched in 1812. Following Molson's lead, the St. Lawrence had a reliable, almost daily steamboat service by 1819. In Atlantic Canada, inland paddlewheelers first appeared on the Saint John River in 1816, and rapidly became a dominant feature on that great navigable river with its many tributaries and deep, protected bays. Additional paddlewheelers followed on the region's many other rivers and sheltered coastal waters.

In Britain, steamboats developed differently from those in North America. With a lack of major navigable rivers and lakes, British steamboats were largely built for coastal and ocean voyages. As a result, they were smaller, slower and sturdier than their North American counterparts. They also differed in another key component.

North American steamboats relied on high-pressure boilers for speed, which, given the technology of the time, often blew up. British steamboats, on the other hand, used much safer low-pressure boilers. As a result the British got a head start over the Americans in the development of steam technology for ocean travel.

Sketch of John Molson's Accommodation, *the first steamboat on the St. Lawrence River, launched in 1809.*

The American steamboat Phoenix *made the first open sea voyage from New York to Philadelphia in 1808.*

Ironically, however, the American steamer *Phoenix* made the first open sea voyage during a trip from New York to Philadelphia in 1808.

Fulton undoubtedly copied many of his ideas from Scotsman William Symington (1763–1831), the first person to design an engine specifically for a steamboat. His 25-foot long "pleasure boat," built for Patrick Miller, steamed across a Scottish lake in October 1788, carrying on board one of Miller's tenants, the poet Robbie Burns. Symington followed with the steam tugboat *Charlotte Dundas* in 1802, which towed two 70-ton barges some 20 miles in six hours along the Forth-Clyde Canal. Unfortunately, owners of boats that were not steam-powered, ostensibly concerned over damage to the canal banks by paddlewheel wash, forced *Charlotte Dundas*'s withdrawal from service. Symington later died in poverty.

Painting of the Scottish steamboat Comet, *the first commercial steamer in Europe, on the Clyde in 1812.*

A British steamer, the 43-foot-long, four-horsepower *Comet*, designed by Henry Bell (1767–1830), became the first commercial passenger steamboat in Europe with her inaugural run between Glasgow and Greenock, Scotland, in August 1812, covering the 20-mile distance in three and a half hours. Three years later, in May 1815, the 72-foot-long, 16-horsepower *Glasgow* made the first ocean voyage of any length by a steamboat in Europe. Built in Glasgow, the ship was delivered to her London owners in a roundabout voyage spread over three weeks that covered 760 miles in 121 hours of sailing time. *Glasgow* was not big enough, nor her engine and boiler efficient enough, to carry sufficient coal for the entire journey. Although *Glasgow* had clearly shown that steamboats could undertake long ocean voyages — the first English Channel crossing by a steamer followed in 1816 — it took several more years before long ocean jour-neys made completely under steam power and out of reach of coaling stations were realized.

Sam Cunard did not start out believing in steam. His early opinions of steamboats were shared with his fellow Halifax merchants. Dismissing them derisively as "steam kettles," the uncompromising businessmen allowed that steamers were suitable for inland waterways, but would never replace sailing ships on the open ocean. In fact, the most recent initiative in shipping to catch their attention involved sailing ships: the packet line.

Despite advertised departure dates, ship's captains wait-ed until they had enough passengers and cargo to make the voyage worthwhile. Even when fully loaded, they might have to wait again, until wind, weather and water condi-tions were suitable for departure. Overall, it was a very inefficient system. Passengers wasted time and lost money on lodgings and food, cargoes didn't meet delivery deadlines, perishable goods rotted. In 1817 a group of five New York ship owners led by Jeremiah Thompson started something completely new. Their innovation was to create a "line" of ships across the Atlantic, initially of four, three-masted, square-rigged vessels, which sailed on known dates between New York and Liverpool, whether they were filled or not, no matter what the weather. They called it the Black Ball Line, from a large black ball painted on the fore topsail of each ship. From the first sailing in January 1818, the Black Ball Line quickly established a reputation for speed, comfort and consistency.

Other packet lines followed: Red Star (1822), Blue Swallowtail (1822), Black X (1823), Dramatic (1836), Red Cross (1843) and Boston (1844). Competition brought change. Ship designs, essentially the same for 200 years, underwent rapid transformation in one-tenth that time, resulting in bigger and faster vessels. Passenger facilities were provided to previously unheard of standards. It seemed as if sailing ships were going to be around for a long, long time.

As Sam had diversified his business, he had established a reputation for reliability with local civilian and military officials, and they rewarded him with additional contracts. One such agreement had him provide a sloop for government service in 1815, later upgraded to a brig in the summer of 1817, at Lieutenant-Governor Lord Dalhousie's direction.

Someone unhappy with or jealous of this arrangement complained to the Colonial Secretary in London, Lord Bathurst, that Sam had boasted of making profits of £1,930 on the service, plus an additional bonus because payment was in British bills of exchange. This form of recompense carried a premium of fifteen per cent at the time, due to a temporary shortage of foreign currency, a legacy of the War of 1812.

In 1822, Dalhousie's replacement as lieutenant-governor, Sir James Kempt, was directed to advertise for new tenders. Sam won the contract with the lowest bid, £1,500 annually, and provided the service for another 11 years. As he explained to Kempt, he had no other use for the vessel and did not want to scrap her. Interestingly, the Colonial Office estimated that the annual cost of operating the brig was £1,400.

In a few years, the Cunard fleet and shipping interests had expanded considerably. By 1825 about 30 vessels now carried the new Cunard flag, a sea blue pennant with a big white star in the middle, while the family had partial interest in another 10 or so. These ships sailed to Britain, the West Indies, South America, Newfoundland and United States, carrying cargoes of dried fish, timber, wood products, rum, sugar, hides, coffee, dry goods, food stuffs, flour, raisins, molasses, sheep and horses, in addition to passengers and mail. Sam's family also continued to expand. Susan bore Sarah Jane (Jane) in 1821 and Anne Elizabeth (Ann) in 1823.

One of the most lucrative parts of the growing Cunard business was the Miramichi fish and timber trade. The Miramichi River and its 12 branches drained a vast region of several thousand heavily forested square miles of the colony. The region had only come to the fore during the War of 1812, when its boundless stands of white pine and red spruce replaced Britain's usual supply of wood from the Baltic Sea, cut off due to the war against Napoleon.

Joe Cunard, 12 years younger than Sam, assisted by Henry, ran this section of the firm. They opened an office in Chatham, where they purchased a wharf and a store, and quickly moved into lumbering, milling and shipping. The web of the Miramichi and its tribu-

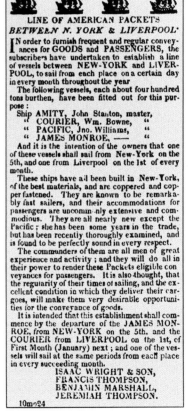

The first advertisement for the Black Ball Line of fast sailing packets between New York and Liverpool appeared in 1817.

taries made their business possible, giving access to the remotest areas and enabling logs to be floated out in the spring after cutting during the winter.

Joe was as ambitious as Sam and had the same inner drive, but the two brothers could not have been more different. Where Sam was small and quiet, Joe was big and boisterous; a mountain of a man over six feet tall and weighing more than 200 pounds. Few individuals had neutral feelings about Joe, and regarded him with a mixture of either admiration and love or fear and hate. Joe was a contradiction. He could be kindhearted one minute and cruel the next, generous at times and grasping at others. He was domineering, yet seems to have craved affection.

Joe ran the Miramichi business like an independent fiefdom. He was extravagant and reckless, a larger than life lumber lord. He often travelled in a coach and four accompanied by two footmen. He also rode about on a huge white horse, a pistol projecting from each long riding boot. Besides supplying Sam with lumber, Joe expanded into other businesses and to other parts of New Brunswick. He estab-

Above: The owner stands outside his home, one of the very few houses in the Miramichi region not burned to the ground in the Great Fire of 1825. The Cunard timberlands also survived the most devastating effects of the fire.
Right: Joseph Cunard, Sam's younger and more flamboyant brother, responsible for the family's business interests on the Miramichi.

lished his own shipyards, mills, brickyards and accounting office, and opened branches at Richibucto and Kouchibouguac in Kent County in 1830 and at Bathurst on the Bay of Chaleur in 1831.

Unlike Sam, Joe did not handle wealth or position well. Even so, he had some of the Cunard luck. He lorded it over his workers and was arrogant in dealing with his business rivals, in particular the firm of Gilmour and Rankin of Douglastown, who leased timberland on the north bank of the Miramichi. On October 7, 1825, after a particularly hot and dry summer and fall, the largest fire ever recorded in the Maritimes and the biggest wildfire ever identified in North America (an unenviable record that still stands) broke out in the Miramichi forests. The inferno was helped along by highly flammable debris from widespread logging operations. By the time the flames burned themselves out, the region was devastated. The fire obliterated over 6,000 square miles, about one-fifth of New Brunswick's forests. Some estimates state that 300 people lost their lives. In addition, the flames destroyed over 500 houses and buildings, killed nearly 900 head of cattle, plus hundreds of other domestic and wild animals, burned crops stored in barns and set ships ablaze. Newcastle, Douglastown and other communities were wiped out.

The Cunard timber leases were south of the Miramichi, an area the fire reached but where the damage was not as extensive as on the north bank. Joe's competitors, Gilmour and Rankin, lost not only valuable uncut timber, but ships, wharves and buildings. The great forests of the Miramichi normally accounted for nearly one-half of all the colony's exports and the fire wiped out huge tracts of the best lumbering region of the province. Although Joe had a head start, the other firms soon caught up to him, and by the 1830s the province's timber industry was booming again.

4 CLIPPERS & CANALS

Expanding his shipping activities and branching out in other areas continued to be Sam's priority. Many people now depended on him for their keep. Besides his own increasing family, he took care of his wife's parents, the Duffuses, and supported his younger siblings until they married or became established.

One of his ventures was in the tea trade. At the time, Britain did not allow her colonies to trade directly with China. All tea destined for British possessions was first shipped from Canton to London by the Honourable East India Company, which held a monopoly on the trade with China, the only place where tea was cultivated at the time. From London, tea was distributed throughout the British Empire. In July 1824, Sam learned that Britain was going to establish overseas agencies to control this distribution. In future, tea would be shipped directly from China to Quebec in East India Company ships, bypassing London, before delivery to the Maritimes. Knowing the problems of navigating from Quebec to Halifax against contrary winds and, for much of the year, through ice, Sam decided to bid on the tea agency for the British Atlantic colonies.

Sam's competitors were also eyeing this business opportunity, an assured moneymaker based on the popularity of tea. Among them was dour Enos Collins (1774–1871), perhaps Halifax's richest merchant. Collins was born in the nearby Nova Scotia town of Liverpool, one of 23 siblings and half-siblings, and went to sea as a cabin boy on one of his father's vessels. In his teens, he captained a schooner bound for Bermuda and at the turn of the century was first

Above: In this nineteenth-century Chinese watercolour, western merchants are pictured buying tea in China.

lieutenant on the famous Liverpool privateer *Charles Mary Wentworth*, cruising the Caribbean trade routes in search of lucrative French merchantmen. When he returned to his hometown, he had enough money to buy part-ownership in a number of ships trading out of Liverpool.

In November 1811, Collins moved to Halifax and set himself up as a shipowner and trader in partnership with Joseph Allison. That same month, he paid £440 at prize auction for a foul-smelling, cramped former tender to a

Spanish slave ship that he promptly rechristened *Liverpool Packet*. While others derided his purchase, Collins had the last laugh. When the War of 1812 broke out, he immediately outfitted *Liverpool Packet* as a privateer. The sleek, black-hulled schooner, her two masts slanted back at a rakish angle, became the most successful privateer in Canadian history, capturing over 100 prizes in 22 months. Collins probably cleared £30,000 from this venture, a hefty boost to his growing wealth. He and Allison, however, made most of their money by purchasing prize ships and their cargoes at auction for rock-bottom prices, then reselling them at a considerable profit.

After the war, Collins also got involved in several businesses, including currency speculation, lumbering and whaling, diversifying in the same way as Sam. Not surprisingly, he approached Lieutenant-Governor Kempt in an effort to secure the same tea business Sam was after, believing his position in the colony would guarantee him the agency. Two years earlier, in 1822, Collins had threatened to leave the colony and take his money with him, but was induced to stay by an offer of a seat on the Council of Twelve, the province's governing body.

Ostensibly, the Crown appointed the Council's members on the advice of the lieutenant-governor, although in reality its members were selected by the colony's most influential people — the ultimate old boys' club. The Council functioned as a sort of Cabinet for the provincial government, with the lieutenant-governor at the top of the pyramid. Collins's appointment was an indication of his stature among Nova Scotia's ruling elite. His position was reinforced in 1825 by his marriage to Margaret Halliburton, eldest daughter of Supreme Court judge (and future Chief Justice) Brenton Halliburton.

Like many of his contemporaries, including Sam, the hard-headed Collins believed in a ruling class, but also believed — again, as Sam did — that it was their responsibility to look after their less fortunate fellow citizens. He was a member of the Poor Man's Friend Society and donated to several charitable organizations.

With regard to the tea contract, Sam outfoxed Collins. Rather than rely on a third party to conduct negotiations and present his case, Sam did it himself. He sailed to England on a mail packet four days before Christmas 1824, reached Falmouth in February, took a three-day coach ride to London and immediately went to the offices of the "John Company" on Leadenhall Street to bid on the contract. In his petition for the contract he noted, "Our pretensions are grounded upon our long residence in the Provinces and a thorough knowledge of the Trade and People, we possess every convenience in Fireproof Warehouses and means to effect the intended object . . . you may rely upon our zeal and attention . . ." Sam got the lucrative contract, but he need not have rushed; it took another five months before it was confirmed.

Right: Enos Collins, a native of Liverpool, became one of Halifax's leading businessmen; Above: Portrait of Collins's Liverpool Packet, *which became the most successful and famous privateer in Canadian history.*

Not being one to waste time, Sam took advantage of his extended stay in London to seek out other business opportunities. The great city was no stranger to him, as he had visited it several times on earlier business trips. Hanging around the Colonial Office, where he knew several officials, was an excellent way to learn about planned and potential government policies for the Atlantic colonies, any one of which might offer a sharp entrepreneur the chance to make some money. He also took the opportunity to visit various merchant bankers and learn their business practices.

The entire story of tea production — growing, picking, curing, packing, selling and loading on ships — is shown in this nineteenth-century Chinese print.

Sam returned to Halifax that summer, sailing from Gravesend in June 1825 on the brig *Susan*, one of his ships. By the time he arrived home, 36 days later, his second and last son, William, was three months old. It was not until the end of May 1826 that the results of Sam's perseverance in London paid off, when the East Indiaman *Countess of Harcourt* appeared off Halifax Harbour with the first shipment of more than 6,500 chests of tea for Cunard, having sailed halfway around the world from Canton. As she reached Cunard's Wharf, a large crowd gathered, alerted by the signal flags on Citadel Hill. On June 19, after three weeks of unloading her cargo, the first quarterly sale of tea at public auction was held at Sam's new stone warehouse close to his wharf.

Sam was soon exporting large quantities of Bohea, Souchong, Hyson and other China teas to New Brunswick and Newfoundland, with smaller amounts to Prince Edward Island and Bermuda, Jamaica, Barbados and Demerara. Some of the tea was carried on Cunard vessels, while ships of other traders distributed the rest. Each fall Sam even sent tea to Forsyth, Richardson, and Company, the agents for the Canadas (present-day Quebec and Ontario) at Montreal, before ice closed the St. Lawrence River for the winter. He usually sold two-thirds as much tea as they did annually.

The establishment of the Cunard tea agency effectively put a stop to the smuggling that previously brought in much of the region's tea from the United States, an illicit trade that had allowed a few to grow rich. Those who suddenly found this lucrative source of income cut off cannot have been too pleased with Sam's actions. The tea auctions continued until 1860, as long as Cunard retained the agency, with Sam usually acting as auctioneer whenever he was in town. The annual arrival of the Cunard tea clipper in Halifax was an eagerly awaited and notable occasion.

The building housing Collins' Bank in Halifax's Historic Properties.

September 1, 1825. Sam subscribed one-tenth of its £50,000 capital.

Before the establishment of the bank, businessmen often personally carried large sums of money — British pounds, American dollars, even Spanish doubloons — because bank drafts, the preferred method of dealing with large sums for business transactions, were virtually unobtainable in the colony. By the mid-1820s mercantile activity in the province had reached the level where it could support a bank and the partners reaped a huge return on their investment. The monopoly provoked frequent negative comments, but most merchants were quite happy with the arrangement. As one of them noted, the bank "put a lot of money into circulation, which offered great convenience to those in trade." Although not the president, Collins was the principal partner in the bank, which was housed in the same stone building on the Halifax waterfront as his company. Locals called it Collins' Bank. The Halifax Banking Company was the only bank in the province until 1832, when the Bank of Nova Scotia received its charter over the objections of Collins.

Sam's commission on the tea was only two per cent, but the quantities involved resulted in large sums of money, which soon became his most dependable source of revenue. Sam always submitted his remittances promptly to London, but starting in 1840 the East India Company had to ask him annually to forward the balance due. Complying soon after being asked, Sam appears to have purposely delayed payment, perhaps using the funds as a ready source of capital to finance his many schemes. Some of the money was likely used to cover his share of the transatlantic steamship line he soon founded.

Typically, Sam had not been idle in the interim and moved into other business ventures. Enos Collins, possibly impressed with Sam's ability to secure the tea agency and obviously not holding a grudge over it, invited Sam to join him, Joseph Allison and five other members of the town's mercantile elite to be a partner in Nova Scotia's first bank. Although Collins had been unsuccessful in several earlier attempts, the Halifax Banking Company (now the Canadian Imperial Bank of Commerce) was formed on

The same year the bank was formed, Sam became one of the shareholders in the Annapolis Iron Mining Company, formed to smelt and manufacture iron in Annapolis Royal (Thomas Chandler Haliburton, a future friend, was a fellow investor). The company secured the mining rights to an old French mine, constructed a stone blast furnace and manufactured pig iron, which was then made into stoves and kettles. Initial doubts about whether the local finished products could compete with English ones, which were turned out more cheaply, proved to be true and the costs soon exceeded any returns. In addition, the largest shareholder, Cyrus Alger of Boston, and his fellow American investors, wanted to sell the pig iron in the United States, while the Nova Scotians wanted to concentrate on finished products. The company folded after an initial £30,000 investment. As a small shareholder, Sam did not lose much money. In any case, this failed venture did not deter his entrepreneurial enthusiasm. Within a few months he was involved with another, bigger project, one that aroused the interest of many Nova Scotians — and one that had a far greater potential for failure.

Above: The ruins of Lock 4, known as Fletcher's Lock, on the Shubenacadie Canal; Right: Shubenacadie Canal Company seal.

The railroad-building fever that hit Europe and North America during the first half of the nineteenth century was soon followed by a building boom in another form of transportation: canals. In the United States, the Erie Canal from Albany on the Hudson River to Buffalo on Lake Erie was completed in 1825. In the same year the Lachine Canal around the rapids at Montreal opened and construction started on the Welland Canal to bypass the great cataract at Niagara.

First suggested by Lieutenant-Governor John Wentworth in 1794, for years many Nova Scotians had talked about a canal joining the towns at the head of the Bay of Fundy with Halifax. Such a canal would replace the hazardous 500-mile, week-long voyage around the rocky, shoal-laden coast of southwestern Nova Scotia with a 50-mile, one-day overland journey. A chain of narrow lakes ran north from Halifax to the Shubenacadie River, requiring, at least in the minds of many, a series of short canals to link them. Engineers, however, estimated 19 locks would also be required to get the ships up and down the hilly terrain.

Investors seemed undaunted by the technical challenges. The twin spirits of progress and optimism dominated the times and £80,000 — £15,000 from the provincial government — was quickly subscribed for the Shubenacadie Canal Company. Sam invested £1,000 and became the company's vice-president. Forty skilled stonemasons and their families were brought over from Scotland to build the locks of solid Nova Scotia stone. The masons may have been experienced in building locks in their native land, but they were unaware of the harsh winters in the colony, especially of the deep penetration of frost into the ground. Each spring saw the previous summer's work damaged by frost heaves, requiring repairs

Above: Portrait of Joseph Howe, journalist, politician, premier and lieutenant-governor; Right: A fine example of the whalers' art of scrimshaw — an etching of the biggest wooden ship ever built in the Maritimes, the square-rigged W. D. Lawrence.

this province and employed for a time of not less than 18 months in the Southern Whale Fishery." Sam's long-held desire to bring the whalers back was well known and with the generous government "bonus" he established the Halifax Whaling Company with himself, Joseph Allison and Lawrence Hartshorne as trustees. Sam and his brothers Ned and Joe headed the joint stock company in which 12 Halifax merchant firms participated.

The newspaperman Joseph Howe (1804–73), one of Sam's friends, was among the most vocal critics of this cozy arrangement, arguing that the men who formed the Halifax Whaling Company were the only ones in any position to take advantage of the bounty. John Howe, Joe's father, was a Loyalist who came to Nova Scotia after the American Revolution and secured employment as the colony's Postmaster General and King's Printer. At age 13, Joe was already assisting his father in these duties. Largely self-educated, he was already developing his verbal skills, having inherited a love of words from his father. Early in 1827, Joe — a sturdy, lively 22-year-old — and a friend purchased a Halifax newspaper and renamed it the *Acadian*.

The Halifax Whaling Company investors did not attempt to deny Howe's accusations in the *Acadian*. They regarded their actions as potentially benefitting the whole colony and believed, as the ones who assumed the greatest risk, they were entitled to a substantial return on their investment. In November 1826, the Halifax Whaling Company launched *Pacific* at Lowden's Shipyard in Dartmouth. Its construction had provided jobs for 25 local men. Outfitted for her three-and-a-half-year voyage, *Pacific* departed Cunard's Wharf in late January 1827, headed for the rich whaling waters of the South Pacific, which were dominated by the Nantucket whalers.

Word reached Sam that *Pacific* had reached northern

before new work could commence. The masons eventually completed two locks, only to see all their hard work destroyed when a dam, intended to hold back the waters of an upper lake, ruptured and washed away everything that had been accomplished. By 1831 the company had expended its capital and collapsed.

Sam tried again to re-establish the whaling industry. He and a number of Halifax's influential merchants pressured the colonial government into offering a £1,500 bounty to "the first two vessels that may be fitted out in

Peru six and a half months after leaving Halifax, and already had 110 barrels of whale oil, better than many of the American whalers who had been out there longer. Later news from the Sandwich (Hawaiian) Islands indicated *Pacific* had a full cargo of over 1,000 barrels of oil. When she returned to Halifax the investors received the government bounty.

Sam dispatched his own whalers in *Pacific*'s wake. *Susan* and *Sarah* sailed in 1834 and 1836, roaming the distant South Pacific islands all the way to New Zealand in search of black and sperm whales. The 375-ton *Rose* departed in 1837, returning two years later with 2,400 barrels of black and sperm oil, only to find the full government bounty of two pounds per ton was unavailable.

Another whaler, *Samuel Cunard*, followed, but did not

Mid-nineteenth-century watercolour of an idyllic scene on the Southwest Miramichi where, along with the Miramichi's other tributaries, the Cunards had vast timber holdings overseen by Joe Cunard.

have the luck of her namesake. In New Zealand, her crew deserted and her captain, not content with drowning his sorrows in drink, jumped overboard and drowned for real. Returning from a second Pacific cruise in 1846 *Rose* made Sam's last whaling voyage. Fortunately, the hold carried a full cargo, but Sam's long-held goal of re-establishing Nova Scotia's whaling fleet never came to fruition.

The Cunard's businesses on the Miramichi continued to prosper, although Sam was concerned about the rate of expansion. In 1838, when Joe added a gristmill to a sawmill he had built three years earlier, Sam grumbled, "I am sorry to find that you have been adding a large building to the Steam Mill. It increases the risk of fire where such an immense property is at stake beside the additional

Capital sunk in this confounded Undertaking."

Initially, Joe commissioned others to build ships for him; but in 1839 he began to build his own and eventually had two yards at Chatham and one each at Bathurst, Richibucto and Kouchibouguac. He constructed at least 75 vessels between 1839 and 1847. Most of the ships were sold abroad and not registered locally, a procedure known as "going home under certificate."

As Joe's finances improved, so did his standing in the colony and he became involved in local affairs and politics. One of his first public duties was as a member of the relief committee established after the Great Fire of 1825 to assist the hundreds of people left homeless. He became a Justice of the Peace, member and chairman of the Board of Health and

Savannah *steams into harbour. In 1819 she crossed the Atlantic in less than four weeks, partly under steam.*

lighthouse commissioner. In 1828 Joe was elected to the Legislative Assembly. He was then appointed to the Legislative Council in 1833 and the Executive Council in 1838, although he does not appear to have been a key figure in any of them. When he joined the Executive Council, Lieutenant-Governor Sir John Harvey described him as "one of the most wealthy and influential merchants in the province."

While the Cunard brothers pursued their various interests and activities, progress continued to be made in the development of steamboats. When initial reports of the first transatlantic crossing by a ship powered by steam reached Halifax in 1819, they aroused much interest and speculation. The 110-foot *Savannah*, an American sailing ship equipped with two collapsible side paddles, made the transit from her Georgia port to Liverpool in 27½ days. In response, a group of New York investors formed the Ocean Steam Ship Company to build transoceanic steamers. However, when all the facts came out, it was revealed that *Savannah* had used steam power (by burning firewood) for only 85 hours and had, in fact, taken longer to cross the Atlantic than the fast sailing packets of the Black Ball Line. The Ocean Steam Ship Company quietly faded from view.

It took a few more years before another bout of steamboat fever broke out. Following rumours in 1825 that the American and Colonial Steam Navigation Company of Britain was about to commence a regular steamship service around the British Isles and once a fortnight to New York via Halifax, a committee was formed in Boston to promote steamship service from that city to Maine and Halifax. The Lower Canada (present day Quebec) Assembly offered a £1,500 subsidy, to which Nova Scotia added another £750, to establish a steamer link between Quebec and Halifax that connected with the Falmouth mail packets. Steamships would shorten the Quebec-Halifax journey from an arduous and dangerous month-long sailing voyage to a week or less, and some Halifax businessmen believed their town — closer to Europe than any American port — could become the major ocean terminus in the Western hemisphere.

A group of London businessmen attempted to raise £50,000 for the Quebec and Halifax Steam Navigation Company, but when reports began to circulate that some published steamship triumphs were not all they seemed to be (for example, a report in 1825 that the British steamship *Enterprise* had sailed from London to Calcutta in 113 days was later tempered by the fact that she only spent 64 days under steam), the fever broke and disappeared rapidly. The naysayers had a field day, crowing that they had always known steamships could not make long journeys, as no ship was big enough to carry the amount of coal needed for transoceanic voyages. The Boston firm put aside its plans to run steamers to Halifax, and the Quebec and Halifax Steam Navigation Company failed, as it did not attract sufficient investors on either side of the Atlantic.

When steamship service was initiated between Boston and Portland, Maine in 1826, Joseph Howe grumbled in the pages of his newspaper, "It does seem a strain upon our enterprise, that upon the harbours or estuaries of this Province we have yet received no advantage from the most gigantic improvement of modern times — navigation by steam." Howe, later a champion of human rights, was an

early champion of the steamship and frequently wrote of the advantages that steam brought to ships. He noted the ease with which steam tugs could tow vessels out of port, no matter which way the wind was blowing. Howe applauded the growing number of steamers on British rivers and coasts, including the latest coaster, *United Kingdom*, a 175-foot-long "stupendous vessel," powered by two 100-horsepower engines built by Robert Napier of Glasgow, who would later build Sam's first steamers. *United Kingdom* boasted a large gentlemen's sleeping room and a ladies' cabin that contained "every convenience that luxury could invent."

Although Howe was frequently critical of Sam in public, in private they remained the best of friends. Eventually, Howe's goading would be in part responsible for the revolution wrought by Cunard in transoceanic shipping. Yet, initially, Sam did not share Howe's enthusiasm for steamships. When some Pictou businessmen tried to obtain his support for their steamer proposal in late 1829, he dis-

Stock certificate in the Halifax Steam Boat Company signed by Samuel Cunard.

The Dartmouth-Halifax steam ferry Sir Charles Ogle, *launched in 1830.*

missed them. "We are entirely unacquainted with the cost of a Steam Boat," he wrote, "& should not like to embark in a business of which we are quite ignorant & must therefore decline taking any part in the one you propose getting up."

Sam was, however, rapidly becoming aware of the possibilities that steamboats offered, and had seen several in operation in Britain and America. He observed their capabilities first hand when a steam ferry, *Sir Charles Ogle* began chugging daily across the harbour between Halifax and Dartmouth in 1830, replacing a horse-powered one. While still in his twenties, Sam had become one of the original directors of the Halifax Steam Boat Company when it was formed in 1815, and eventually became its president in 1836. With his business connections, he was instrumental in purchasing a steam engine from England to power a second ferry, *Boxer*, launched in 1838. Under his presidency, shares in the company rose from five shillings to £105 by 1842.

But before steamships took hold of Sam's life, he had other things on his mind. While *Pacific* was being outfitted in January 1826 to sail to the South Pacific in search of whales, Sam applied to Lieutenant-Governor Kempt to lease the Cape Breton coalmines for 30 years at £6,000 annually, plus a royalty of two shillings per chaldron (approximately 36 bushels) on shipments over 60,000 chaldrons. He specified that Sydney must be made a free port and its wharves and breakwaters improved. Kempt supported Sam's bid and forwarded it to the Colonial Office, noting "The Messrs. Cunards are Persons of Considerable Capital quite equal to carry on this Establishment & perfectly acquainted with the Country." Despite this support, Sam's bid failed. The British government awarded the rights to mineral exploitation in the colony to the General Mining Association (GMA). The best Sam could do was to win the contract in 1827 to provide wharf and warehouse space in Halifax for the GMA, succeeding over the long-established firm of Belcher, Binney, and Company, on the recommendation of the GMA's engineer. It took a few more years, but eventually Sam became the GMA's agent. But first there were other paths to follow.

5 STATESMEN & STEAM

Sam's successful business enterprises pushed him up the ladder of colonial Halifax society, much of which was centred in the town's mercantile elite. Now that he was one of them, several of Halifax's major businessmen convinced him to enter politics. In April 1826, he agreed to stand for a seat representing Halifax County in the Legislative Assembly. The Assembly, the lower house of the provincial government, was comprised of men of property who were elected by other men of property. Although the Assembly was representative it had no real power, and any of its decisions could be overturned by the upper house, the Council of Twelve.

Halifax's Province House, as painted by J. E. Woolford.

On the day Sam was to declare his intentions in the Legislative Assembly of Province House, he stood up and read a few words from a piece of paper he took from his pocket. After noting he had come forward not of his own accord, but at "the written request of the Merchants, and other respectable inhabitants," he stated, "I had no ambitious views to gratify, no objects to attain, the good of the country was the sole consideration which induced me to assent to their request." Declaring that he objected to candidates and voters wasting three weeks campaigning at such a busy time of year for farmers and fishermen, he withdrew himself as a candidate and sat down.

It was a rare public statement by Sam, a shy man who preferred to work behind the scenes, relying on the support of family rather than political cronies. "I have always been in the habit," he confided later, "of looking after my own business." Politicians had to work the hustings, glad-handing crowds and making frequent public appearances and speeches. Sam did not like crowds, and he was even less inclined to speak in front of them. He may also have been conscious of his lack of formal education, compared with his business peers and other leading men in the colony, a deficiency that would have been highlighted if he had to make frequent speeches inside or outside the Legislative Assembly.

Left: A view of sailing ships and dinghies in Boston Harbour; Right: Halifax lawyer William Blowers Bliss.

Sam's supporters were dumbfounded, although some of them suspected the real reason for his action had nothing to do with farmers and fishermen. Halifax lawyer William Blowers Bliss (1795–1874) speculated, "I believe the real cause to have been that he grew nervous and frightened and timidity got the better of his judgment." He also noted, "His conduct is strange and has done him no good." Bliss, himself elected to the Assembly in 1830 and appointed a Supreme Court judge in 1834, was part of the colony's ruling elite. He backed the establishment of the Bank of Nova Scotia in 1832 and became one of its first directors. While Bliss may have been right about Sam's timidity, he was dead wrong about its effect. Sam's surprising refusal caused him no harm in the end.

Attending to his many business interests required Sam to travel frequently. He could be found in Pictou, the Miramichi, Boston, New York and London, or aboard ships either coming or going. Perhaps because of this constant travel, he probably realized the great advantage steam offered to ocean travel, an idea that may have begun to work away in his mind at this point. Although his business and related travels consumed much of his time, he still assumed several civic duties in an era where part of the measure of members of the upper classes depended on doing good deeds — usually for the lower classes. In addition to the Poor Society and Sun Fire Company, Sam served on committees for the Public Library, Mechanics' Institute and Lighthouse Commission.

As he was pondering his current and future business endeavours and civic duties, Sam also attended to family matters, which held some tragic events. He and Susan took in Hannah, the daughter of his cousin Tom Murphy, when Tom's wife died. Hannah helped fill the void left by the death of little Susie, who would have been only three months older than Hannah had she lived. Sam had been educating his oldest son Ned in the various Cunard businesses since he was 10, and often took him on his visits around the Maritimes or to New England. Sam's last two children were born at this time, Isabella (Isabel) in February 1827 and, less than a year later, Elizabeth in January 1828. On February 2, 1828, 10 days after having borne Elizabeth, her ninth child, Susan Cunard died, leaving Sam a widower at 40. Although it was usual at the time for men in such circumstances to remarry, Sam never did.

The Cunards and Duffuses immediately stepped in to help Sam bring up his eight surviving children, ranging in age from a new-born infant to 12 years old. Susan's mother, 56-year-old Susannah Duffus, wanted the children to move in with her, but Sam convinced her that a better arrangement was for them to remain in their own home under a capable housekeeper. Susannah continued to act as an advisor to the household, a role she had filled even when Susan was alive.

Although Sam was not religious, the family worshipped regularly at nearby St. George's Round Church. On his deathbed, when his son Ned asked him if wanted the services of a minister, Sam replied that he "did not feel and admit and believe." Now when Sam travelled around the Maritimes, he usually took three or four of the children with him. Sometimes the whole family came, especially when he went to the Miramichi to visit Joe and Henry. Joe was still unmarried, but Henry had married Elizabeth

St. George's Anglican Church, known as the Round Church.

Duffus and bought a small country home on the river. Their cousin, Hannah Murphy, who had been taken in by Sam and Susan when Hannah's mother died, now went to live with Henry and his new wife.

In 1830, with a personal fortune estimated at £200,000, making him an important member of the mercantile community, Sam was appointed to the Council of Twelve, taking his seat on November 6. A Tory supporter and very much a man of his time, Sam supported the form of government that ran the colony, believing that ordinary people were incapable of choosing the people to govern them. Coming only four years after he withdrew as a candidate for election to the Legislative Assembly, his appointment was a clear indication of his acceptance by the highest ranks of the colony's ruling oligarchy, a relatively closed group based largely on family background and connections, frequently reinforced by strategic marriages. Inherited wealth was also a factor, but occasionally, as in the case of Enos Collins and Sam, inclusion could be based on the wealth created by self-made entrepreneurs. Appointment to the Council brought with it the advantages offered by powerful connections in any age: patronage appointments, government contracts, privileged information and investment opportunities.

Sam joined the Council just as the system was beginning to show cracks, hastened by Joseph Howe's critical editorials in his current newspaper, the *Novascotian*. Even so, Howe praised Sam's appointment and expressed the hope that "the same liberal and expansive views which have distinguished Mr. Cunard as a merchant, may be observable in his legislative character. He is wealthy and influential — he need fear no man, nor follow blindly any body of men; and we trust that he will not disappoint the hopes which many entertain of the benefit to be derived from his weight in the counsels of a branch, that, at the present moment, is really in no good odour throughout the Province."

While the spirit of reform was being felt in Britain, it still had a long way to go in Nova Scotia. On a trip to London on government business, Sam and two other council members wrote home that Britain itself was in danger of collapsing over the Reform Bill then before Parliament. "Everybody," they noted, was "lamenting the necessity of sacrificing the established institutions of the country and yielding to the popular voice, instead of rousing themselves to oppose it like Englishmen."

In 1830, before Sam was appointed to the Executive Council, the Assembly of Lower Canada had doubled its subsidy for a Quebec-Halifax steamship service to £3,000, while Nova Scotia again offered £750. As potential investors considered this proposal, Sam formed a committee in Halifax to obtain stockholders and managed to get himself elected its head in March. The committee was successful in attracting sufficient numbers of small investors, who made up the majority of those interested. Sam proposed that each shareholder — no matter what the amount of his investment — would have just one vote in any proceedings. The subscribers in attendance then voted him local agent for the company, with the powers of general management and financial control. With over 200 shareholders in Quebec and the Maritimes, and a capital of £16,000, the Quebec and Halifax Steam Navigation Company was launched. Now it needed to launch a ship.

The contract to construct a steamship was given to Quebec shipbuilder George Black, a shareholder, and merchant John Saxton Campbell. Fellow Quebecer James Goudie, who had apprenticed under a Scottish shipbuilder on the Clyde, was the designer and construction foreman. He based his design on four steamers he had worked on in Scotland, and whose plans he had brought back with him. The keel was laid on September 2, 1830, and the ship was launched on April 27 of the next year, at Cape Cove, Quebec, below the monument marking the spot where Wolfe fell in 1759.

The 1,370-ton SS *Royal William* (named after the ruling monarch, William IV) was 160 feet long and 44 feet wide, a large steamship for the time. Like other steamships of her era, she was essentially a sailing ship fitted with an auxiliary steam engine. She carried three masts, schooner-rigged, and had a tall stovepipe funnel and a paddlewheel on each side. It was not until about 1850 that vessels were built as steamships first and equipped with auxiliary sails.

After launching, *Royal William* was towed upriver to Montreal where a 200-horsepower, two-cylinder engine and a crankshaft, both built in Scotland, were fitted. She cost £16,000. *Royal William* sailed to Halifax on August 24, with 20 cabin passengers (at six pounds and five shillings each, including a berth and meals), 70 in steerage, a little freight and 120 tons of coal. She called at the Miramichi on the way, where Joe Cunard was her agent as well as a shareholder, and Pictou.

An artist's depiction of the launching of the Royal William *at Quebec in 1831. Sam became the Halifax agent for the ship's owners.*

When *Royal William* docked at Cunard's Wharf on August 31, six and a half days after leaving Quebec, Sam, just arrived from Boston on *Emily* with Ned in tow, was there to greet the new venture. The ship's engineer, J.G. Denter, later recalled that Sam visited the ship several times while docked and inquired about her speed, sea-keeping abilities and coal consumption, making notes of several pertinent points. Sam was impressed with and proud of the ship he had helped see through fruition. In England earlier that year, Sam had experienced his first train ride on the new Liverpool and Manchester Railway. He drew a parallel between railroads and steamships, and said *Royal William* convinced him that "steamers properly built and manned might start and arrive at their destinations with the punctuality of railway trains on land . . . . We have no tunnels to drive, no cuttings to make, no roadbeds to prepare. We need only build our ships and start them to work."

Sam wasn't the only one whose interest was fully aroused by the steamship. The *Acadian Recorder* waxed effusively, "Her beautiful fast sailing appearance, the powerful and graceful manner in which her paddles served to pace along, and the admirable command which her helmsman had over her, afforded a triumphant specimen of what steam ships are."

Sam immediately ordered a steamship for his own fleet,

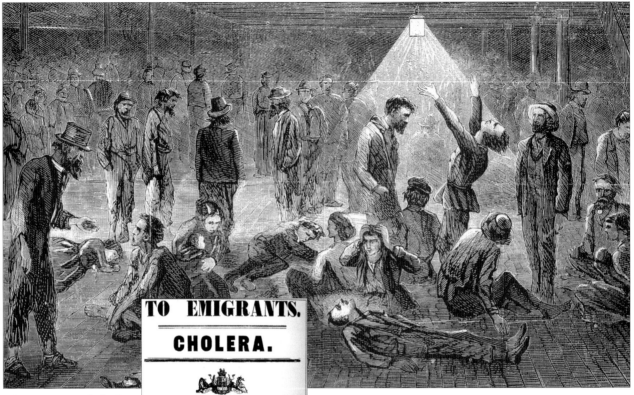

TO EMIGRANTS.

CHOLERA.

CHOLERA having made its appearance on board several Passenger Ships proceeding from the United Kingdom to the United States of America, and having, in some instances, been very fatal, Her Majesty's Colonial Land and Emigration Commissioners feel it their duty to recommend to the Parents of Families in which there are many young children, and to all persons in weak health who may be contemplating Emigration, to postpone their departure until a milder season. There can be no doubt that the sea sickness consequent on the rough weather which Ships must encounter at this season, joined to the cold and damp of a sea voyage, will render persons who are not strong more susceptible to the attacks of this disease.

To those who may Emigrate at this season the Commissioners strongly recommend that they should provide themselves with as much warm clothing as they can, and especially with flannel, to be worn next the Skin; that they should have both their clothes and their persons quite clean before embarking, and should be careful to keep them so during the voyage,—and that they should provide themselves with as much solid and wholesome food as they can procure, in addition to the Ship's allowance to be used on the voyage. It would, of course, be desirable, if they can arrange it, that they should not go in a Ship that is much crowded, or that is not provided with a Medical Man.

By Order of the Board,

S. WALCOTT, SECRETARY.

Colonial Land and Emigration Office, 9, Park Street, Westminster, November, 1853.

*Above: A portrayal of sick steerage passengers during a transatlantic crossing;
Right: A notice from a Liverpool immigration office warning passengers about cholera.*

to use on the weekly mail run between Pictou and Charlottetown, for which he had just received the contract. While this Cunard ship was being built in England, *Royal William* made two more round trips between Halifax and Quebec before ice closed the St. Lawrence for the season. Her owners considered sending her overseas for the winter, to work the English coastal waters and earn more money;

but in the end she was laid up at Quebec. Capital was a problem. *Royal William*'s first season's takings were modest, although the somewhat immodest charges for passengers and freight had been the subject of several complaints.

The start of the 1832 season saw *Royal William* offering greatly reduced rates in order to draw more customers. Unfortunately, her first sailing was delayed until June 16 because of an outbreak of the feared and highly contagious cholera at Quebec. Caused by the consumption of water or food contaminated by waste, a major epidemic began in India in 1827, made its way to Britain by 1831, and entered North America the next year from European immigrants arriving on ships via the St. Lawrence River. At the time, infected individuals were quarantined while the disease ran its two-to-seven day course, ending in either recovery or, as frequently happened in pre-antibiotic days, death.

When *Royal William* reached the Miramichi on 19

June, she flew the dreaded yellow flag that meant only one thing: cholera. Apprehensive local authorities immediately quarantined the ship. Ironically, Joe owned Middle Island, later the site of a quarantine station for arriving immigrants. Three weeks later, *Royal William* sailed for Halifax. On the way, landing was denied at Pictou by an armed vessel, and upon arriving in Halifax the ship was quarantined again. It was mid-August before *Royal William* returned to Quebec, where she was laid up once more. The steamer had made only one round trip during the whole season, a severe financial blow to her shareholders. The Quebec and Halifax Steam Navigation Company went bankrupt.

The owners blamed each other. The Quebec group pointed the finger at Sam, accusing him of asking too much for his services as the agent in Halifax and for not working amicably with them. For his part, Sam blamed the Quebec group. Writing to Nova Scotia's Provincial Secretary, Sir Rupert George (in his typical, rushed, unpunctuated style), he noted that *Royal William* "was neglected in the Winter and the frost burst the Pipes & otherwise injured the Machinery by which means a great expense was incurred and the sailing of the Boat delayed until the 15th June whereas she should have made two or three trips before that period." He also objected to the provincial bounty being paid to the Quebec group "in consequence of the Boats only making one trip during the whole Season." In his opinion, they had already received more than they should have, all of which was lost due to their actions, as well as "the object in view frustrated."

Royal William was sold at a sheriff's auction in Montreal in the spring of 1833 for £5,000, some £11,000 less than the cost to build her two years earlier. Her new owners, which included some of the previous ones, sent her on a coastal voyage to Boston — the first British steamship to enter the harbour, where U.S. President Andrew Jackson inspected her. Then the new owners decided to send *Royal William* to Britain to be sold again.

The partners believed *Royal William* was the first ship to cross the Atlantic by steam alone, but the 105-foot steamer *Cape Breton*, which the GMA had purchased for their coal-mining operations in Sydney and Pictou County, had

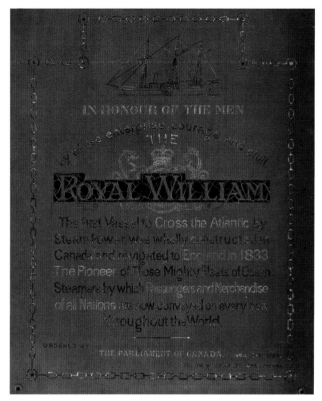

The whereabouts of this Royal William *commemorative brass plaque, unveiled in 1864 by direction of the Parliament of Canada, remains unknown.*

already crossed the ocean, arriving in Sydney 14 days before *Royal William* departed Pictou. Other steamships had also accomplished similar feats. The French steam warship *Caroline* sailed from Brest to French Guiana in 1824, and the little Dutch steamer *Curacao* had already made three return crossings between Antwerp and the Dutch West Indies (now the Netherlands Antilles) between 1827 and 1829, a fact virtually unknown outside of Holland. *Royal William* did enter the record books, however, as the first steamship to sail from Canada to Britain.

Before making the transatlantic crossing, *Royal William* steamed to Pictou to take on coal, much more than her captain, John McDougall, would have liked: "We were very deeply laden with coal, deeper in fact than I would

ever attempt crossing the Atlantic with her again." McDougall sailed from Pictou on August 18, 1833, with 36 crewmen, seven passengers and 324 tons of coal. Her cargo included "one box of stuffed birds, six spars, one box, one trunk, some household furniture, and a harp."

Royal William made the crossing to Cowes on the Isle of Wight in 19 days. At times McDougall thought they might not make it. On Newfoundland's Grand Banks a terrific gale broke the top off the foremast and knocked out one of the engine's two cylinders. Then the engineer reported they were sinking. "Things looked rather awkward," McDougall later wrote in a classic understatement, "however we managed to get the vessel cleared of water, and ran by one engine after the gale." Every fourth day they proceeded under sail while the engine was shut down to clean out salt encrustations from using seawater in her boilers. This common problem was solved in 1834 by the invention of surface condensers, which provided fresh distilled water for ships' boilers. After repairs and painting at Cowes, *Royal William* went on to London and was sold to Spain for £10,000 in 1834. With a battery of guns installed and rechristened *Isabella Segunda*, she became the first steam warship in the Spanish Navy and the first steam vessel ever to fire a shot in action.

Royal William's successful passage showed that steamships were capable of undertaking transatlantic journeys; they could carry sufficient coal and did not need the right winds to keep going. Engine reliability obviously required improvement, but that would certainly come with time. What was needed now was someone with the vision to pursue the concept of regular transatlantic crossings by steam.

If Sam learned anything from his experience with *Royal William*, it was the importance of not having to rely on others in business, of being able to make the key decisions himself. Although approaching middle age and quite wealthy, he still possessed the determination and single-mindedness to accomplish any task he set for himself. He was not ready to sit back and let the world pass him by; there were still new fields to conquer — and money to be made.

Top: A 1933 rendition of Royal William *departing Pictou for London a century earlier in 1833; Above: Crossing the English Channel on a paddle steamer during a storm.*

Painting of Royal William, *1834.*

Sam presented a dilemma to the Halifax elite. His wealth and appointment to the Council signalled his place in the highest level of local society, but his educated and cultured peers still regarded him as a social outsider, not quite one of them. In 1831, Halifax lawyer Lewis Bliss (brother of William Blowers Bliss) wrote to another brother and lawyer, Henry, in London, and asked him to welcome Sam on a trip to Britain. Henry acted as one of two agents for Nova Scotia and New Brunswick, charged with supporting legislation favourable to the colonies, opposing unfavourable legislation and attempting to see that the views of the provincial authorities were known at the Colonial Office.

Bliss's letter provides an interesting word picture of Sam: "I think he may be called a gentlemanly man," he opined, "— very polished he cannot be expected to be having I believe received a scanty education, and moved for the early part of his life not so much in the *higher circles* now thrown open to him. He is the most liberal as well as the most extensively engaged in business of all our Merchants. He certainly is mild & pleasant in his manners — of an apparently equal temper, and possesses a gentle and not inharmonious voice — in short I look on him as a very good kind of man, and if not very pleasant & agreeable very far from the reverse. He may be said to be modest — free from pride & affectation, and I think ambition, or if ambitious, not manifesting it in his conduct at all turns & on all occasions." Bliss's portrait of Sam is an accurate description of how he was viewed by the Halifax oligarchy. Yet, in one area, Bliss seriously underestimated his subject.

An oil painting of Charlottetown, the capital of Prince Edward Island, in 1834.

Sam still harboured the ambition and drive of a younger man. The next few years would show just how much.

In 1832 Sam put a new English-built steamer on the Pictou-Charlottetown-Miramichi mail run. *Pocahontas* ran for a year before he leased her to the GMA. Sam replaced her with the larger *Cape Breton*, which he leased from the same company. Subsequently, Joe purchased *Cape Breton* and she became the first steamship to be wholly owned by the Cunards. *Cape Breton* remained a Cunard ship until 1842, when she returned to England and was converted to

a sailing ship. In 1846 Joe built *Velocity*, the first steamer constructed on the Miramichi.

Joe Cunard was busy moving forward in his life. He married Mary Peters, the daughter of Judge Thomas Peters, in 1833 and bought a house in Chatham the next year. He remodelled and enlarged it and furnished it with crystal chandeliers from Europe and custom-made furniture from Boston. Its garden was the size of a city block. Peacocks paced its perfect lawns. Joe Cunard was an important and powerful figure on the Miramichi.

At the same time, Sam was serving his first years on the Council. He faithfully attended meetings and was active on committees, especially those concerned with commerce. His actions were always motivated by what he thought would be best for business. His commercial interests expanded. He became a director of the Bank of British North America and agent for the GMA. One of his next ventures involved land on Prince Edward Island, an endeavour which would cause as much frustration as it brought benefit.

During an extended business trip to England in 1837–38, influential Halifax lawyer and politician George Renny Young (1802–53) contacted Sam about forming a Prince Edward Island land company. Young represented a number of absentee landowners in their attempt to avoid any loss of their lands for non-payment of taxes and for failing to meet the settlement terms of their original grants. Land ownership on the Island had developed in a unique way from the rest of the country. When the Island became an English possession at the end of the Seven Year's War in 1763, it was the first of Britain's new territories to benefit from a plan to survey North America.

By 1765 Surveyor General Samuel Holland had divided the Island into 67 townships of 20,000 acres each. Almost all the townships were granted through a 1767 lottery to military officers and others to whom the Crown owed favours (one noble, the Earl of Egmont, even asked to have the whole island granted to him!). There was virtually no Crown land. Owners were required to settle their properties, but few made any effort to do so. As a result large areas of the Island remained undeveloped, and those who wanted to farm had to pay steep rents or purchase fees. Many owners refused to sell their land in any case, and immigrants found they had no more security of tenure in the New World than they formerly had on their holdings in Britain.

The revenue to administer the Island was to come from taxes collected from the proprietors, but they were often impossible to collect. Any attempt to enforce the terms of the grant were usually overruled by the British government, under the influence of the landowners, most of whom never set foot in the colony. Confrontation between the proprietors' agents and the tenants were common, frequently resulting in violence. All efforts to change the system continued to be blocked in England. George Young was a part of yet another delegation, making representations to the Colonial Secretary, Lord Glenelg.

Young persuaded Sam to join him in forming a joint stock company called the Prince Edward Island Land Company. Other members were Young's father-in-law, Thomas Brooking, and the Earl of Selkirk's agent, Andrew Colvile, with a local board comprised of Young, Sam and Joe Cunard. The company purchased the 60,000-acre Hill estate for £10,000, and acquired the mortgage on the 102,000-acre Cambridge estate for £12,000. Sam and Joe each held three-tenths of the shares, Colvile two-tenths and Brooking and Young one-tenth each.

Young was the son of merchant John Young, who under the pen name "Agricola" wrote several well-respected essays in the *Acadian Recorder* from 1818–22 on the need for agricultural reform in Nova Scotia. "Agricola's" writings came to the attention of Lieutenant-Governor Lord Dalhousie, himself a keen farmer, and resulted in the establishment of several agricultural societies across the province dedicated to improving farming methods. In 1824 George Young started his own weekly newspaper, the *Novascotian*, unique among the colony's papers because of the large amount of local material. Young quickly established the *Novascotian* as the best newspaper in Nova Scotia, and then in December 1827 sold it for £1,050 to 23-year-old Joe Howe — who made it one of the leading newspapers

George Ramsay, the ninth Earl of Dalhousie, lieutenant-governor of Nova Scotia from 1816 to 1820.

in British North America. By 1834 George and his brother William had set up a law practice. William was a political opportunist who became Premier in 1859 (Joe Howe was his Provincial Secretary, and followed him as Premier when Young became Chief Justice of Nova Scotia the next year). He was also one of Halifax's main benefactors and was knighted in 1869.

While in England in 1837–38 acting for his PEI landowner clients, George Young married Jane Brooking, daughter of Thomas Holdsworth Brooking, a man of some substance who held elitist and authoritarian views. Young attempted to get himself appointed to Nova Scotia's new Legislative Council while in England, but was rebuffed. He enlisted his father-in-law's help with the Colonial Secretary, but he too was unsuccessful, leading to unfounded suspicions of a conspiracy against Young.

On the land question issue, Young received assurances from Lord Glenelg that no action would be taken to confiscate the lands of the absentee landowners. Young then proposed the plan to establish the Prince Edward Island Land Company, in which the owners involved would unite their properties in a large-scale immigration scheme. Sam and Young visited their estates in August 1838 and discussed the land tax with the colony's lieutenant-governor, Sir Charles Augustus FitzRoy, assuring him they "wanted a common line of policy between the Proprietors and their tenants calculated to restore peace and to promote the prosperity of the Island."

A dispute between the company's shareholders broke out almost immediately. At a meeting in Charlottetown on October 20, relations between Sam and Young soured over a disagreement about the appointment of the resident land agent. Sam wanted to give the job to James Horsfield Peters, a New Brunswick lawyer who had married his eldest daughter, Mary, in 1837. Young wanted his brother, Charles, to have it. With the Cunards as the majority shareholders, Sam exercised his authority and refused to discuss the matter further; Peters moved to the Island in 1838 to manage the estates. Sam then bought out Young and the other partners in March 1839.

Sam's actions had two results, one short term and one long term: he had overextended himself financially, leaving him cash-poor, deeply mortgaged and needing to rely on others for financial backing; and he had made enemies with a powerful Halifax family, one that had a long memory. George Young's mother, Agnes Renny Young, cautioned him about Sam's "immense" power: "People fear him so much that they will keep quiet and submit," she warned. "He never was friendly to our family and will give you a blow where he can." Thomas Brooking was so upset over Sam's treatment of his son-in-law that he hoped for "an opportunity to tell him in person."

As the decade progressed, Sam became less active in Nova Scotia politics. The Council was coming under increasing attacks from the Reformers led by Joe Howe. In 1838, when the Council was divided into executive and legislative branches, Sam was asked to remain on the new Executive Council, but he attended fewer and fewer meetings. In 1840, the new Lieutenant-Governor, Lord Falkland, asked Sam to resign from the Council to make room for Reformers in a coalition government, much to the indignation of the Tory press. Sam willingly obliged and was permitted to retain the title of "Honourable." Enos Collins also left the Council and withdrew from active politics, although he continued to provide financial backing to the Tories. For Sam, the idea of a transatlantic steamship line had taken hold in his mind by now, and that is where he directed his considerable energies and talents.

6 PROPOSALS & PARTNERS

As the 1840s approached, significant advances had been made in steam technology. Improvements in engines, boilers, crankshafts, paddles — and in the ships that they would power — enabled engineers to design steamships specifically for transoceanic travel. Three English companies had entered the unofficial race to be the first to complete such a ship. In 1837 three giant wooden side-wheelers were taking shape, built to withstand the rigours of the North Atlantic. In Bristol, the Great Western Steamship Company's luxurious *Great*

Western was the first to start construction under the direction of the most brilliant engineer of his — and perhaps any other — time, Isambard Kingdom Brunel (1806–59). On the Mersey, the smaller *Liverpool* was taking shape, while the mammoth *British Queen* lagged behind on the Thames.

Great Western won the construction race. She departed Bristol for New York

Right: Isambard Kindgom Brunel stands in front of the massive launching chains of Great Eastern, *1857; Above: Lithograph of Brunel's* Great Western *on her maiden voyage in 1838.*

on April 8, 1838. Junius Smith, an expatriate American living in England, who had founded the rival British and American Steam Navigation Company in 1835, which was building *British Queen*, still unfinished on the stocks, was not prepared to let the Great Western Company beat him. He chartered the 178-foot *Sirius*, a vessel half the size of *Great Western* built for the London-Cork run.

Sirius sailed from Cork on April 4, four days before *Great Western* departed. *Liverpool*'s owners, the Transatlantic Steamship Company, were also forced to charter a ship, coincidentally named *Royal William*. Even smaller than *Sirius*, she was never a contender, but did establish two records: the smallest passenger ship to steam the whole way from Britain to America, and the first vessel ever to cross the Atlantic under continuous steam power.

Sirius won the race across the Atlantic and reached New York first on April 23, nearly out of coal and having burned some of her wooden furnishings — according to legend — to keep up steam. *Great Western* was only 12 hours behind, having made the fastest crossing ever from Britain to America in an impressive 15 days and five hours. In addition,

upon arrival 30 per cent of her 660 tons of coal was still left in her bunkers, enough to convince the most ardent disbelievers in the efficacy of steam. New Yorkers were agog at these twin achievements and talked of little else. *Great Western* became the first recipient of the fabled Blue Riband, a notional symbol emblematic of the fastest ship on the North Atlantic.

Three mornings later word of the exploits of *Sirius* and *Great Western* reached Halifax on the Royal Mail packet *Tyrian*, a 10-gun brig. That night, *Tyrian* sailed for Falmouth with more passengers than usual, several of them bound for Queen Victoria's coronation. Among them was Joseph Howe, who had been elected to the Legislative Assembly the previous year as a Reform candidate, and was finally fulfilling a long-held desire of visiting Britain and the Continent.

Howe's election followed a famous libel trial brought against him after he published a letter on New Year's Day, 1835, accusing the Halifax magistrates of misconduct. Despite having broken the criminal libel law of the day, Howe studied law for a week — no lawyer gave him a chance of winning — and successfully defended himself. In a courtroom presided over by Chief Justice Brenton Halliburton, Howe's masterly six-hour speech won the jury to his side and established his reputation as an orator. His victory was also a key signpost on the road to a free press. More importantly, his success was an early and positive step towards responsible government for the province, a cause to which Howe devoted himself. Howe championed the view that the elected representatives should have the power to run the government of the colony. When this

Sirius, the first steamship to carry mail across the Atlantic.

Above: The "other" Royal William is shown in this lithograph battling across the Atlantic during a voyage to New York in 1838, establishing a record as the smallest passenger ship to steam the whole way across; Right; Thomas Chandler Haliburton, lawyer, judge, politician and author.

reform was achieved in 1848, Nova Scotia became the first British colony to win the right, in no small measure due to Howe's part in the struggle.

Accompanying the Reformer Howe on this voyage was his good friend, life-long Tory Thomas Chandler Haliburton (1796–1865), the Chief Justice of Common Pleas for the colony, better known as the creator of the Yankee clock peddler and wit Sam Slick. Howe had already published two of Haliburton's books, *An Historical and Statistical Account of Nova Scotia* (1829) and *The Clockmaker; or The Sayings and Doings of Samuel Slick, of Slickville* (1836). His assistance in facilitating the publication of *The Clockmaker* helped Haliburton to garner an international following that rivaled Dickens's for a short time.

On May 16, becalmed by a sudden loss of wind a few hundred miles from the English coast, *Tyrian*'s passengers sighted a distant plume of smoke astern and speculated whether it was from *Sirius* or *Great Western*. The arguments were soon settled as *Sirius*, two weeks out of New York, pulled alongside. Not knowing how long he would be becalmed, *Tyrian*'s captain decided to send the mailbags ahead with *Sirius*, which would likely make Falmouth within two days.

Howe managed to get a seat on the rowboat taking the mail across and spent "five minutes of chat with the passengers on the quarterdeck and took a glass of champagne with her captain in the cabin." The experience exhilarated him, and he considered the future for steamships: "Now that the experiment has been fairly tried, there can be little doubt that ere long the Atlantic will be aswarm with these sea monsters, and that a complete revolution will be wrought in the navigation of the ocean, as has already been witnessed on the rivers and inland seas." He also considered their potential: "immigrants would come out" and, with government subsidies, "the public mails and dispatches could also be forwarded . . . at much less expense than the present dilatory and costly system."

As *Sirius* took her leave and disappeared over the eastern horizon, Howe, Haliburton and their fellow passengers from the Maritimes discussed the possibilities. They estimated the British government could send the mails to Halifax on a steamer at about half the cost of the Falmouth packets, and resolved to do something about it. They did. On arrival at Falmouth five days later (and 25 days out of Halifax), Howe and Haliburton journeyed to Bristol to ask the Great Western Steamship Company to consider calling at Halifax once a month, while a New Brunswick passenger, William Crane, visited the British and American Steam Navigation Company, owners of *British Queen*. Haliburton later claimed that his visit to Bristol made him the "instigator of steam transit across the Atlantic."

Howe went on to London on May 29 and found Sam at his Piccadilly hotel, where he was waiting with his son Will for their ship to load at Gravesend. Over dinner that evening, Howe briefed Sam on the results of the visits: The Great Western Company was prepared to put ships on the Halifax route, "provided the British government would give them the carriage of the mails." The British and American Steam Navigation Company was also interested. Sam sailed for home the next day. It took more than a month to reach Halifax, a voyage that gave him ample opportunity to consider the possibilities offered by steamships. By the end of the trip, he had resolved to do something about it.

The introduction of transoceanic steamships followed a major revision in the way the British government distributed the mails to Ireland and Europe. In 1833 the authorities had switched from crown-owned shipping to private steamship companies to carry the post, in exchange for an annual subsidy. With an eye to potential future wars, all contracts with private steamship companies contained a clause requiring mail boats to be leased to the Admiralty to carry soldiers if hostilities broke out. As a result, in 1837, the packet service was made the responsibility of the Admiralty, under a newly created position — the Comptroller of Steam Machinery and Packet Service. The first Comptroller was Edward Parry, now Rear Admiral Sir Edward, Sam's old friend. Parry was contemplating using steamships for the transatlantic mails.

When Sam arrived in Halifax, he immediately set about trying to raise enough capital to build three or four steamships to carry passengers and mail across the ocean. Thus armed, he intended to approach Parry with a plan to transport the post between England, Halifax and the United States for a fixed annual fee. He proposed to use his hometown as the western terminus, with auxiliary steamers taking the mail to and from either Boston or New York, a change from the sailing packets, which went all the way to New York. The new route would enhance Halifax's position — and his own — for British trade with America. He also considered the mails for Canada, still carried overland through New Brunswick in the summer and through Boston in the winter. The railroad under construction between Boston and the Hudson River would mean faster mail delivery to Canada, resulting in demands to use Boston year round.

Ships at a New York pier with the Blue Swallowtail packet Leeds *closest.*

To ensure Halifax's place in the system, Sam included mail service to Quebec as part of his proposition.

Now that he had a plan, Sam needed financial backing before he could pitch it to Parry. Recent years had not been good ones for business. Since taking office in Britain in 1830, the reforming Whigs had been unable to sort out the country's finances, resulting in a series of annual deficits. This situation and other factors led to a period of economic misery, high unemployment and deep depression, which began in 1837 and lasted until 1843. The effects of this economic crash were felt in Nova Scotia. Money was tight.

Sam's recent purchase of one third of the shares of the Prince Edward Island Land Company had not helped his overall financial situation. He approached his Halifax merchant associates, many of whom he had done business with or collaborated with in other enterprises in the past, for assistance. Not one of them was prepared to gamble any money on what they considered a risky undertaking. Some even advised against it, especially in view of Sam's unsuccessful whaling and PEI land speculation ventures. The new native-born generation of Halifax merchants, who had replaced members of the older generation on their death or retirement and now dominated the local business scene, proved to be just as cautious as their predecessors.

During the summer of 1838, as Sam

George Burns, one of Sam's key partners in the transatlantic steamship venture.

continued to try to raise money, there was a sudden drop in the amount of mail carried to Halifax by the Falmouth packets because *Great Western* was proving to be a much faster option. Sam turned to his old friends in Boston in an attempt to interest the merchants of that city in his proposal, but he met with the same results as in Halifax. If anything, the Bostonians were even more convinced than their Haligonian peers that transatlantic steamers were a passing fad, and a dangerous one to boot. Boston ship owners were more interested in maintaining and increasing their share of the lucrative Atlantic clipper ship market. Rather than steamships, they spoke only of improved sailing ships, faster and better appointed than those now plying the ocean. It was the wrong time and place for Sam to drum up support for his steamship idea. He returned to Halifax, perhaps a bit wiser, but no richer or closer to his goal.

Meanwhile, in Britain, Parry had contacted George Burns (1795–1890), a Glasgow ship owner, asking him if he would be interested in bidding on the contract. Burns was not. The canny Scot already had a profitable coastal steamer service between Glasgow and Liverpool and was not prepared to engage in the still unproven possibility of regular, year-round, transoceanic steamer crossings. Parry went public.

On November 8, 1838, the following announcement appeared in the London *Times*: "Steam vessels required for conveying Her Majesty's Mails and Dispatches between England and Halifax, N.S., and also between England, Halifax and New York." By the time this information reached Halifax on the Falmouth monthly packet, it was two weeks past the December 15 bid deadline. Furthermore, the monthly service proposed was to commence in April, departing from Bristol, Falmouth, Liverpool or Southampton. Clearly, the Admiralty did not want to consider bids from the colonies, or from companies that did not already have steamships in operation.

Two British companies submitted bids. The St. George Steam Packet Company proposed starting at once with its fleet of coastal steamers, but was not prepared to risk its vessels in a North Atlantic winter. The Admiralty rejected its bid.

A few passengers and crew from a sinking packet ship are rescued from rocky ledges off the coast of Ireland, while their unfortunate companions cling to the ship in this dramatic artistic portrayal.

The Great Western Steamship Company, so far the only company that offered regular transatlantic steamship service (*British Queen* was still unfinished, and would not be ready until the summer of 1839), made a counter proposal to the Admiralty. *Great Western* had been steaming away faithfully and made five round-trip crossings in 1838, which not only proved the feasibility of steamships, but also showed the shortcomings of the Falmouth packets, commonly known as "coffin brigs" because of their many sinkings, taking crew, passengers and mail with them. So many foundered that people usually took the precaution of sending several copies of letters by different vessels to make sure at least one copy got through.

As *Great Western* had shown the need for larger ships, in the range of 1,200 tons and 450 horsepower (the Admiralty tender had specified at least 300 horsepower) the Great Western Steamship Company pleaded that it needed more time. The company offered to build three such ships within 18 to 24 months to carry the mail. In return, they asked for £45,000 a year for seven years. The Admiralty, however, wanted action in the spring, not two years later. On January 10, the Lords rejected the Great Western bid, the same day that the *Novascotian* in Halifax reprinted the Admiralty's original advertisement.

Unaware of the Great Western Company's rejected bid, Sam intended to make his case for the contract. Despite being well past the bid deadline, and without the necessary financial support for his scheme, he boarded the packet *Reindeer* to Britain. Two months after the closing date for tenders he reached his destination.

What possessed Sam, at 51 years of age, to embark on such an uncertain and untried venture? While it was true that a steamship had successfully crossed the Atlantic on a more-or-less regular basis, none had yet done it during the winter months, when the North Atlantic was at its most fearsome. Sam had no fleet of steamships, no money to build them, and no partners with whom to share the risk. All he had was a vision — an "ocean railway" — and the passion to pursue it, plus supreme confidence in his own abilities.

It should have come as no surprise that Sam followed the path that he did. Ships and shipping had been his life, and he knew them intimately. He also had some experience with steamships, dating back to *Royal William*. He had more first-hand knowledge of transatlantic crossings and their dangers than most, having made many tedious voyages on the packets.. "I came home in those ships very frequently," he later said, "and I have lost a very great many friends in them." Even as Sam sailed eastwards, the westbound Falmouth packet simply disappeared ("went missing" was the euphemistic newspaper term), swallowed up somewhere in the vast North Atlantic, further evidence of his belief that "The Atlantic to America is the worst navigation in the world. The westerly winds prevail very much, and you have ice and fog to contend with."

Given the uncertainties of steamship travel and the state of the current ships capable of making the crossing, Sam probably hedged his bets that no company was prepared to commit to a year-round regular contract before bringing improved ships into service. The time this action required gave him a chance to compete on an equal footing.

Sam carried a letter from Nova Scotia Lieutenant-Governor Sir Colin Campbell to the Colonial Office, reminding them that Sam was "one of the firmest supporters of the measures of the Government" and that his position as "one of the principal Bankers and Merchants," as well as other appointments, gave him "a great deal of influence in this community." With his GMA, tea agency and eastern seaboard mail

contract connections, Sam was not unknown in British corridors of power and the letter may have been redundant; but Sam was not taking any chances.

In London he proceeded to his Piccadilly hotel and used an office in nearby Ludgate Hill. When he learned the Admiralty had rejected the only two bids received and had extended the closing date, he must have felt elation — and confirmation of the suitability of his vision. In quick succession, Sam met and discussed his plan with key individuals involved in the contract: Charles Wood at the Admiralty, Francis Baring at the Treasury, Edward Parry at the Comptroller of Steam Machinery and Packet Service. Sam had taken the Admiralty tender and improved it. Instead of monthly sailings, he offered a weekly service.

Sam spent hours discussing his proposal with Wood and Baring, making adjustments, revising calculations, checking routes. The biggest change was reducing the service to twice monthly, more than the Admiralty intended, but less than Sam proposed. The details were agreed on verbally by the time he submitted his formal offer on February 11: "I hereby offer to furnish Steam Boats of not less than three hundred Horse power to convey the mails from a port in England to Halifax and back twice in each month. Also to provide branch boats" of half that horse-power "to convey the mails to Boston and back to Halifax. Likewise to provide boats ... to convey the mails from Pictou to Quebec and back" during the navigation season. With an eye to the future, he added, "Should any improvements in Steam Navigation be made, which the Lords of the Admiralty may consider as essential to the Service, I do bind myself to make such alterations and improvements as their Lordships may direct." He asked for £55,000 annually for 10 years to make 24 round trip crossings (£10,000 more than Great Western had asked for half that number), promising to start on May 1, 1840.

To clinch the deal, Sam still needed signed contracts for building ships and engines. What followed was one of the most fruitful partnerships of the Age of Steam, one that set the tone for the Cunard Line during its formative years and well beyond.

7 *BRITANNIA* & BOSTON

Sam spoke to James Cosmo Melville, a friend and secretary of the East India Company, for advice on British steamship builders. Melville directed Sam north to the Glasgow firms of Robert Napier (1791–1876) and John Wood, who had built the steamers *Berenice* and *London* for the company's East Indian trade, as well as designing the engines for *British Queen*. On February 25 Sam wrote to William Kidston, a friend and business associate in Glasgow (whose company had a branch in Halifax), asking him to obtain estimates from Napier and Wood for one or two ships of 800 tons and 300 horsepower, to be built in 12 months and "pass a thorough inspection and examination of the Admiralty."

Establishing the style of his steamships for years to come (in marked contrast to the luxuriousness of his future American competitors), Sam stressed that he wanted "a plain and comfortable boat, but not the least unnecessary expense for show. I prefer plain work in the cabin, and it saves a large amount in the cost." Napier expressed interest in the project and Sam travelled to Glasgow in early March to meet the tall, distinguished Scot.

Napier was born into a prosperous family of engineers, blacksmiths and mill-wrights. After an apprenticeship with his father, he set up his own engineering business in 1815. In 1823 he built his first marine steam engines, just 11 years after Bell's *Comet* steamed down the Clyde and revolutionized marine transportation. In 1828 he established the impressive Vulcan Foundry and by the 1830s was regarded as a figure of note in the engineering world.

Stern-faced foremen who worked at Robert Napier & Sons in Glasgow, pictured with their families sometime in the 1850s.

Napier's interest in Sam's proposal was based, at least in part, on two factors. He had definite — and different — ideas on how steamships should be operated, at variance with much of the prevailing thought. Rather than run steamers like sailing ships, which most steamship owners did, Napier believed in using a specialized engine room crew to look after the machinery, working under a qualified engineer, with tools, spare parts and a workshop at hand in case of breakdowns. He also wanted to redeem himself after criticism over delays in his building *British Queen*'s huge engine, now finally finished.

Napier needed Sam almost as much as Sam needed Napier. The two men seem to have sized each other up in a very short time. They liked what they saw and a rapport was quickly established. They shared many of the same personality traits: forthright, hardworking, businesslike, terse, ambitious and controlled. They were also within four years of age, and family played a large part in each man's life.

After taking Sam on a tour of his foundry, where 700 men toiled six days a week amid the deafening noise of metal on metal, turning out engines, boilers, funnels, cylinders, pistons and other pieces of machinery essential to the Industrial Revolution, Napier and Sam got down to business. Sam asked the price for three ships of 800 tons and 300 horsepower. Eager to get the order, Napier quoted a deliberately low price of £32,000 each, or £40 a ton. Sam, crafty trader that he was, could not resist bargaining. He told Napier that, although he thought this was "a fair and reasonable price," he could have the order immediately if he agreed to £30,000 for each ship, or £37 a ton. Napier accepted the offer, but suspected Sam may have outwitted him: "From the frank off-hand manner in which he contracted with me, I have given him the vessels cheap."

Napier soon had second thoughts about the size of the ships and informed Sam that he thought they might be too small for the rigours of the North Atlantic. He had worked out an improved design for 200-foot-long ships of 960 tons and 375 horsepower. His changes increased the cost per ship, but Napier offered to build the larger engines at no extra cost, if Sam absorbed an additional £2,000 for the accompanying structural improvements to each vessel. Napier also believed that four ships were needed to keep to a bi-monthly schedule.

Sam agreed to the increase in size and number and on March 18 he and Napier signed a contract. Sam returned to London on the next mail coach and proceeded to the Admiralty and Treasury with details of the ships, which pronounced them "highly pleasing." When he wrote to Napier with this news, he added a slyly oblique appeal to the Glaswegian's sense of Scottish nationalism: "I have had several offers from Liverpool and this place [London] and when I have replied that I have contracted in Scotland they invariably say 'You will neither have substantial work or completed in time.' The Admiralty agree with me in opinion the Boats will be as good as if built in this Country and I have assured them that you will keep to time." Sam's letter had the intended effect. "I am sorry that some of the British tradesmen should indulge in speaking ill of their competitors in Scotland," Napier replied, "I shall not say more than court comparison of my work with any other in the kingdom."

For all his bravado, Sam was in dire financial straits. He needed to come up with £128,000 to build the four steamers, £10,000 of which was required immediately, half for a binder and half for the first installment. Sam also needed an additional £14,000 to finalize the purchase of Young's PEI land holdings. It could not have come at a worse time. Sam's credit was in doubt, so much so that Glasgow banker Robert Rodger only reluctantly accepted Sam's first note to Napier after some delay. The Scot was unnerved and expressed his concerns to the Nova Scotian: "The truth is, had I not been completely satisfied beforehand from other trustworthy sources of your undoubted respectability and highly honourable character, my confidence in you would have been shaken."

Napier was not prepared to let the matter, or his standing — and Scottish pride — rest on a shaky foundation. He confided to banker Rodger, "The transaction with Mr. Cunard is of such a magnitude that I must not have the least risk of trouble or anxiety about the money part of it." The two men devised a plan to raise sufficient working capital locally to cover startup costs and initial operating expenses. His personal engineering reputation and that of his country was at stake, and Napier was not about to see himself or Scotland embarrassed.

Napier discussed Sam's plans with George Burns and the MacIver brothers, David and Charles, who had been running coastal steamers between Glasgow and Liverpool for about 10 years. Former rivals, their partnership had produced a profitable operation in the City of Glasgow

Robert Napier's Lancefield shipyard was one of the firm's many sites in the Glasgow area. The troop ship Malabar *is pictured docked there in 1867.*

Steam Packet Company. Napier advised Sam that the involvement of Burns and the MacIvers in the project would "save much trouble to all concerned and make money" and, contrary to his usual practice, might even entice him to take a "small interest" in the venture. Playing the coy suitor, Sam replied, "I have several offers but am bound to no one," adding "I should much like to have you and your friends with me." The investment of Napier, Burns and the MacIvers attracted others to the venture. Napier's reputation and proven ability to build powerful, reliable engines was a significant factor in this response. Initially, 33 shareholders raised a total working capital of £270,000, later increased to £300,000.

Sam put up the largest amount — £61,000. James Donaldson, Glasgow's foremost cotton broker, invested £18,000 and 11 others contributed between £10,500 and £13,000. Napier and Burns provided £7,500 each, while the MacIvers provided £5,500 apiece. Sixteen smaller investors, including businessmen from Liverpool and Manchester, provided the remainder.

In March 1839, Sam had written to some Boston friends, outlining his dealings with the Admiralty. On April 22, the day after his letter arrived, a number of Boston merchants met in the Tremont Bank and resolved to ask Sam to convince the Admiralty to deliver the mails directly to Boston, rather than by branch boats from Halifax. To help persuade him, the Bostonians offered Sam "a suitable Pier and Dock . . . for a term of two years . . . free from expense to the owners of the steamers . . . ."

Their letter put Sam in a quandary. He wanted Halifax

Boston would be the western terminus for the line. It was the first time he consciously made a decision that relegated his hometown to second place.

Joe had followed his brother to England. Although there is no evidence to suggest he played a part in any of the negotiations with the Admiralty or Napier, he certainly would have liked to participate. He admired his brother's business dealings, conducted on such a grand scale when compared with his activities on the Miramichi. When Joe returned to Halifax on the April packet he immediately informed everyone he could about the mail contract, as if it

Above: Trees were felled in the winter and hauled by teams of oxen or horses to the nearest tributary of the Miramichi River, there to await the spring breakup so they could be floated downstream to a sawmill.
Left: The British General Post Office notice announcing the inauguration of Cunard's packet service to carry the mails to North America.

NOTICE TO THE PUBLIC,

AND

Instructions to all Postmasters.

MAILS for NORTH AMERICA

GENERAL POST OFFICE
June, 1840.

to be the western terminus for his steam packets because of the extra business it would mean for his firm in the trade between Britain and America. In a company with other shareholders, he now had to consider additional factors and look at the bigger picture. Boston was a larger city than Halifax (85,000 versus 20,000 population) and would provide more passengers and freight than Halifax. Loading his steamships in Boston made more sense as it would eliminate the time-wasting and costly transfer of cargoes and people in Halifax. Then there was the Boston offer of free dock use. There were no other Halifax investors in his company to insist on his home city's role in this promising new service. Sam sided with the other shareholders;

were a *fait accompli*, with service starting in about a year. His news excited the townsfolk. The prospect of scheduled steamship arrivals and departures twice a month was a coup. Even New York could not boast of such an arrangement. Local newspapers gushed: "A new era will commence in provincial prosperity from the moment the first steam packet reaches Halifax," one of them predicted, "and no one who knows the superior position of our port but must be convinced that the time is not far distant when it will become the centre of steam navigation for the whole North American continent." Another added, "Thousands will visit us in search of business or pleasure." Excitement ran so high over the expected influx of travellers that a group of merchants banded together and raised the money to build a new luxury hotel.

Joe returned to the Miramichi, spending his last night

before reaching Chatham in nearby Richibucto. He sent word ahead that he had received the orders in England for six new ships. He mentioned the mail contract — leaving people to assume he had secured it. He also announced his expected arrival time in Chatham so that he could be welcomed in style. With 1,500 men depending on him for their livelihood (they were not paid in cash, but in goods from the company's store), Joe was not disappointed. Signal fires were lit, cannons fired, church bells rung and friends rode out on horseback to meet him. A parade

Above: Liverpool's Custom House overlooking the city's busy quays; Below: The Cunard Line crest.

and address of welcome rounded out the day. The next night his praises were toasted at a public dinner where he was the main speaker. Joe did not have Sam's reticence when it came to making speeches.

When the mail contract was finally signed with the Admiralty in June, the size of the ships had again been increased at Napier's intervention: "I cannot and will not admit of anything into these engines but what . . . is sound and good," he proclaimed. Although Sam was initially reluctant to agree to another increase, Melville told him, "The adoption of Napier's views is imperative. He is the great authority on steam navigation and knows much more about the subject than the Admiralty."

The terms specified four steamships, driven by 400-horsepower engines, each capable of carrying 115 cabin passengers. They would sail from Liverpool, with its unrivalled 200-acre dock system on the Mersey, twice a month, calling at Halifax on the way to Boston, then reverse the

voyage, all for a subsidy of £60,000 a year for the next seven years, starting in May 1840. It was a good deal for the Admiralty; operating the sailing packets had cost them more than that annually. It was also the first major instance of a government subsidizing the operations of a private commercial firm.

Napier built the engines for all four ships, but to meet the short deadline the construction of the ships was shared between four Clydeside shipbuilders. The new line was called the

The British and North American Royal Mail Steam Packets Britannia, Acadia, Caledonia *and* Columbia, *Cunard's first transatlantic steamships, are shown in this work by British painter William John Huggins.*

British and North American Royal Mail Steam Packet Company, but it quickly became known as Mr. Cunard's Company or the Cunard Line. It took 30 years before the name was officially changed to the shorter version. By the time Sam sailed for Halifax on *Great Western* in July, the MacIvers were supervising the building of a new terminal in Liverpool, while the four steamships were under construction on the Clyde.

The four ships followed Sam's basic criteria for their construction — plain and comfortable. Their names, judiciously chosen to represent the regional beginnings of the line, were the first in a long line ending in "ia" or "a". *Acadia*, built by John Wood, was used as the pattern for the others. Wood was noted for creating graceful, well-propor-

tioned hulls, "a consummate artist in shipbuilding," as distinguished contemporary naval architect John Scott Russell remarked. The 1,150-ton wooden ships were 207 feet long, 34 feet wide and driven by conventional paddlewheels. They could sustain a speed of nine knots. Three other firms constructed *Britannia*, *Caledonia* and *Columbia*. All four were built for rapid conversion to troopships in case of war, a stipulation of the Admiralty contract, and were entitled to bear the title "Royal Mail Steamer," abbreviated to R.M.S.

These ships were practical answers to the problems posed by the North Atlantic. They incorporated the latest lessons learned, without venturing into risky, unproven technology, a characteristic that became a hallmark of the Cunard Line. Change was incremental, not innovative, such as Napier's engine improvements, which resulted in steam pressure nearly double *Great Western's*, produced more power from less coal, and were introduced over time.

Paddlewheelers quickly brought a lasting change to a ship's layout and its terminology. For example, the traditional aft quarterdeck proved useless as a place from which to command a steamer, especially during the tricky phases of entering harbour and docking, as the paddlewheels and funnels blocked the view. An open catwalk was added to connect the two paddlewheel sponsons, enabling the captain to move quickly from one side to another while manoeuvring in port; the origin of the modern ship's bridge.

Back in Nova Scotia, Sam was hailed as "the colonist... who had the courage to grapple with an undertaking so vast as the carriage of mail by steamer between Halifax and the Mother Country." Sam was clear in his own mind about his part in the process. Glossing over how close he had come to not obtaining the necessary financial backing, he observed, "I had the whole interest for sometime in the original contract...but circumstances turned up which made it necessary that I should part with some portion, and I did; but I still have the management." He was more modest about his involvement in building the ships: "I dare say I get a good deal of credit for it, but I am not entitled to it," he remarked later. "Any credit that there may be in fixing upon the vessels of proper size and proper power is entirely due to Mr. Napier, for I have not the science myself; he gave me the dimensions."

A huge open-air reception and picnic was held for Sam on McNab's Island, at the harbour's entrance, in honour of his winning the contract. Appropriately, the harbour steam ferries *Sir Charles Ogle* and *Boxer* provided transport for the guests to and from the island. Sam quickly became immersed in the arrangements for the arrival of the first of the steamships and port facilities were built or improved at Halifax, Pictou, Boston and Quebec.

Excitement ran high in Halifax, even though there was universal disappointment over the loss to Boston as terminus. Once the mail arrived at Halifax, that destined for Quebec was carried overland to Pictou and loaded on

Unicorn, a Glasgow-built steam coaster that Sam purchased from George Burns, who had used it on the Glasgow-Liverpool run.

While in Pictou in September, arranging docking facilities, Sam participated in the opening of the GMA's not-yet-finished six-mile-long railroad from the pithead of their Albion Mine to Pictou. The first steam locomotive in the Atlantic Provinces, *Samson*, had been shipped in parts from Newcastle-upon-Tyne in May, along with two others, *Hercules* and *John Buddle*. Reassembled in Nova Scotia, *Samson* spent opening day running along the completed portion of the line, carrying mine officials, miners and their families. That evening, at a dinner party, more toasts were drunk to Sam than to the men who built the railroad. Everyone knew that each time his steamships stopped at Halifax they would be filled with GMA coal, coal that Sam got cheaply.

Although *Britannia* was launched in February 1840, she would not be ready for sea by May 1, the date stipulated in the contract. The three other vessels sat in the stocks, even further behind. For every 12 hours departure was delayed, the line was liable to pay a fine of £500, a

An 1839 watercolour of the entrance to Pictou Harbour.

A painting of Britannia's *first crossing of the North Atlantic in July 1840.*

stipulation that would soon eat into their subsidy. A missed sailing was even more severe: an astronomical £15,000. Sam began to have second thoughts about his contractual obligation to provide two monthly sailings during the winter, when longer sailing times would require five ships to meet the schedule. He returned to London in April 1840 and went to Parry with his problem.

Parry agreed with Sam's concerns and wrote to the Admiralty, supporting Sam's request to sail only once a month from December through to February, and asking, "no deduction be made from the amount of Mr. Cunard's contract." In his submission to the Admiralty, Sam stated that "steam boats had not crossed during the Winter and I was therefore quite ignorant of the risk and danger I had to encounter indeed I was very hasty in making the arrangement," while claiming, "In the

Winter Season there is not much commercial interest, and no passengers." The Admiralty approved his request for a reduced winter service, but cut his annual subsidy by £4,000 and insisted that the fines for late summer sailings would still stand. *Britannia* was now two months behind schedule; an interim solution was desperately needed.

The answer to Sam's predicament was *Unicorn*, the coastal steamer purchased for the Pictou-Quebec feeder service. Sam's son Ned was slated to sail on her delivery voyage to Halifax in May. The little steamship carried Cunard's new house flag — a blue pennant with a white St. Andrew's cross near the hoist and a narrow red streamer beneath it — and the first transatlantic mails for the Cunard Line. Ned and 26 other passengers left Liverpool on May 16. After a particularly rough crossing, *Unicorn* was seen on June 1 off the Sambro Light at the outer entrance to Halifax Harbour. The townsfolk turned out in force to greet the arrival of the town's first transatlantic steamship: "The wharves were jammed with people cheering as if at a great victory; guns fired, flags waved, and during the ship's brief stop at Halifax no less than 3,000 Haligonians went aboard for an inspection of this marvel of the age."

After disembarking about half its passengers, *Unicorn* sailed for Boston late that night. On board were several members of the Cunard and Duffus families. The reception that greeted *Unicorn* and Ned in Boston was bigger and better than Halifax's. A flotilla of escorts accompanied them up the bay and crowds thronged the waterfront; cannons roared out salutes and church bells pealed a rousing welcome. That night Ned was feted at a large banquet at which poet Henry Wadsworth Longfellow was the main speaker.

As *Britannia* neared completion at Liverpool's Coburg Dock, Sam and his associates drew up the rules that would guide their ships' captains in their jobs and make the line justifiably renowned for safety. In fact, the line's motto became "Speed, Comfort, and Safety." Based on Napier's ideas, deep inside the ship, a chief engineer supervised the operation of the engine room and its qualified personnel. High above the upper deck, lookouts would be on continuous duty, ever vigilant for other ships and icebergs.

These measures were put into effect on *Britannia*, a two-decker with officers' quarters, galley, bakery and cowshed (cows were carried for fresh milk) on the upper deck, and passenger cabins and dining saloon on the lower one. A tall red funnel topped by a black ring (an identifying signature of future Cunarders) towered amidships, between huge paddlewheels. Like all steamships of the day, *Britannia* was fully rigged for sail, both to take advantage of wind to assist the engines, and as a concession to passengers' concerns about engine reliability.

Each eight-by-six foot, two-person stateroom had two bunks, a settee and a commode containing a basin, water jug and chamber pot for each passenger. Clothes were hung on four coat hooks. A hurricane candle near the porthole provided light. Bed linens were changed on the eighth day, while the two towels per passenger were changed every other day, "or as often as required." Every morning before breakfast the cabins were swept and carpets removed and shaken. Smoking below deck was strictly forbidden and the hallway candles were extinguished at 10 o'clock each night. The saloon contained only the bare necessities for dining, although it was outfitted in good taste.

At 6:00 pm on the evening of Saturday, July 4, 1840 (the significance of the date would not be lost on Americans), *Britannia* steamed away from Liverpool bound for America. Huge crowds thronged the waterfront and small craft sailed beside her. On board were 93 crewmen and 63 passengers, including Sam, his daughter Ann and her friend Laura, Thomas Chandler Haliburton's daughter.

Unlike *Unicorn*'s 16-day voyage, the weather was good and *Britannia* steamed into Halifax in the pre-dawn hours a little over 12 days later. The townsfolk, roused by the pre-arranged signal of a cannon shot, were taken completely by surprise, fully expecting *Britannia* to take at least 14 days to make her journey. By the time the official reception committee scrambled out of bed and hastily

Britannia, *as shown in this painting, was launched in 1840, and secured Cunard's place in history.*

assembled, Long Wharf was already crowded with curious inhabitants, waiting to tour the ship.

The vessel's most important passenger was nowhere to be seen. Sam had already disembarked and gone home to enjoy breakfast and share the latest news with his family, including the engagement of Sam's 19-year-old daughter Jane to 30-year-old Captain Gilbert Francklyn of the 37th Regiment (eventually, of the five Cunard girls who married, all but one wed Englishmen, two of them army officers, and left Halifax for good). Sam thought Francklyn "a very good man," despite the fact he owned no property.

The civic reception committee arrived at seven o'clock and started their speeches. Before they were half over, a messenger appeared with information from Captain Woodruff that he would sail in half an hour. The grandiose plans for a reception were abandoned; the best that could be arranged was a few flag-bedecked ships to escort *Britannia* out of the harbour. She steamed away at nine o'clock, bound for Boston, leaving Haligonians disappointed and wondering what all the rush was about.

After *Britannia* departed, other ships swung into action to deliver the mails left at Halifax. *Unicorn* departed at noon, with the mail for Quebec. Upon return, the steamer docked at Pictou, her new homeport, to ply the Pictou-Quebec route. The Cunard mail brig *Lady Paget* left for Bermuda on the mid-afternoon tide, while a non-Cunard vessel sailed for Newfoundland, initiating a new government-subsidized mail service to that island.

Britannia reached Boston at 10 o'clock the next night, Saturday, to a much more tumultuous reception. Tuesday was proclaimed "Cunard Festival Day," to honour Sam and his achievement, which all Bostonians believed would proclaim their city's

The loving cup presented by the citizens of Boston to Samuel Cunard.

superiority over rival New York. Sam received 1,873 dinner invitations during his first 24 hours in the city. A mammoth parade, led by civic and government dignitaries from all the New England states, started the public celebrations, which ended with a huge dinner for 2,300 people in a temporary pavilion set up for the purpose. Leading citizens made grandiose speeches and toasts, a standard element of official gatherings at the time. The keynote speaker and the country's most renowned orator, Daniel Webster, made an eloquent — and much too long — speech, while the president of Harvard proposed a toast to "the memory of Time and Space: famous in their day and generation, they have been annihilated by the steam engine."

When Sam stood up to acknowledge the the accolades, he gave his usual short and pithy reply, "altogether unused to speechmaking," as he claimed. The highlight of the celebrations was the presentation of a massive silver loving cup, two and a half feet high, paid for with $5,000 raised by public subscription. The ornate gift, known ever since as the Boston Cup, was displayed for years in *Queen Elizabeth 2*. It can now be seen in *Queen Mary 2*, one of the most magnificent cruise ships ever launched.

Britannia sailed for Halifax on August 3, the darling of the New England press. ("Never since the arrival of the Pilgrim Fathers have the shores of America experienced so important an event," in the overblown words of one journalist.) After taking on mail and a few passengers, she steamed off to Liverpool a few hours later, at the same time as *Acadia* left Liverpool for Halifax. As *Britannia* left Halifax, the flag-bedecked warship HMS *Winchester* fired her cannons in salute to the first of Sam's line of regular steamships.

In his hometown, the celebrations for Sam were more subdued than Boston's, the highlight being a scroll signed by several thousand of his fellow citizens. The Haligonians' cheerfulness must have been somewhat forced to cover their disappointment. Not only had Halifax been superseded by Boston as Cunard's western terminus, *Britannia* stayed in Boston for two weeks, but only managed a few hours in Halifax. Even so, a new era in transatlantic travel had begun, and Halifax, if not central to it, was at least a key component.

8 COMPETITION & CARTEL

By the end of January 1841, all four Cunard steamships — *Britannia*, *Acadia*, *Caledonia* and *Columbia* — were in operation and quickly established new records for transatlantic crossing times. Within a year of *Britannia*'s maiden voyage, they maintained peak average speeds of 10 knots westbound and 11 knots eastbound, leaving *Great Western*'s achievement in their wakes. In their first two years of operation, their average crossing time was 13 days, six hours to Halifax, and 11 days, five hours to Liverpool. Boston and Halifax proudly boasted they were the only North American ports with a regular year-round steamship connection with Europe.

Great Western, *Liverpool*, *British Queen* and her new sister ship, *President*, called at New York, but only irregularly. Without set schedules or the cachet of carrying the Royal Mail, they lost business steadily to the Cunard Line. However,

A lithograph commemorating President*'s first voyage in August 1840 showing details of her interior.*

Portrait of Judge Thomas Chandler Haliburton in 1853, three years before he left Nova Scotia and moved to England.

not everyone was ready yet to concede that steamships were superior to sailing ships. Many people still regarded crossing the Atlantic by steamship as dangerous, akin to risking one's life on an expedition into the darkest realms of Africa.

Sam's initial competition soon fell by the wayside. *President*, launched by Junius Smith's British and American Steam Navigation Company, was twice the size of the Cunard steamers and a third larger than *British Queen*. At 2,360 tons and 540 horsepower, the ship reached new heights in mass, muscle and magnificence. Although she was an imposing vessel, her engine was underpowered for her size. Her broad, short shape also mitigated against speed. *President*'s two transatlantic crossings in the summer of 1840 were so slow that her first two captains were replaced. On her second voyage from New York, *President* actually had to turn back for

more coal, arriving at Liverpool 10 days late. The steamer was then laid up for two months during the winter and refitted before her third trip in February 1841, during which she achieved her slowest time yet. *President* departed New York for Liverpool on March 11, overburdened with cargo and coal, carrying 110 passengers and crew. On the second day, she was observed struggling through heavy winter seas off the New England coast. The ship was never seen again. The vast North Atlantic had simply swallowed *President* up. Her sinking was the first transatlantic steamship tragedy; it would not be the last.

President's disappearance affected the whole transatlantic steamship industry. Her owners were forced out of business and sold *British Queen* to a European concern. *Liverpool*'s owners suffered a similar fate. Besides the sailing packets, *Great Western* remained as Sam's sole competition — and she too was in financial trouble. Desperate, her owners attempted to obtain part of the Cunard mail contract from the government in 1846. The authorities, quite happy with Sam's service, stayed with him. The next year, *Great Western* was sold for the West Indies trade. Sam had won the transatlantic steamship competition — at least for the present.

One of those who sailed on *Great Western* in 1839 was Judge Haliburton, returning from his 1837 trip to Britain and the Continent (Howe had returned to Nova Scotia separately in 1838). Haliburton published his experiences the next year in *The Letter Bag of the Great Western; or, Life in a Steamer*. Ostensibly to advertise the advantages of steamship travel, Haliburton's cheap humour and frequent use of racial stereotypes probably deterred many from travelling that way. Haliburton enjoyed the trappings that position and wealth brought, and was extremely class-conscious; in short, he was a snob. Travel by steamship was a great leveller at the time, forcing people from different social classes into a confined space for extended periods. "Steamers carry a mob," he proclaimed in 1854, "and I detest mobs." Yet, in later years, Haliburton maintained he was one of the leading and earliest advocates for steamships, even claiming he was responsible for Cunard seeking the Royal Mail steamship contract.

With large numbers of the public still unconvinced of the safety of steamships, Sam did everything possible to build a reputation for a safe, reliable service. In the spring of 1841, two months after *President*'s disappearance, *Britannia,* inbound from Boston to Halifax, suffered a near tragedy. In charge of a local pilot, she struck a reef off the Sambro Light on the western approach to Halifax Harbour in dense fog. Her captain backed her off and proceeded to Cunard's Wharf to offload his passengers. Although *Britannia* had suffered little damage and was not leaking, because of the recent *President* disaster Sam sent the ship to Saint John for a complete inspection. Only when she was pronounced sound did *Britannia* return to Halifax to pick up her passengers and complete her voyage to Liverpool.

Britannia *in a North Atlantic gale in 1842, as depicted by American painter Fitz Hugh Lane.*

In January 1842, 18 months after her maiden voyage, *Britannia* carried Charles Dickens (1812–70) from Liverpool's Coburg Dock to Halifax and Boston. Her most famous passenger wrote what became the most famous account of a nineteenth-century transatlantic ocean voyage by steamship, published as *American Notes*. Dickens, only 30 years old and already an author with an international reputation, was not impressed, and his description of the ship and its facilities spares nothing.

His "state-room" was an "utterly impracticable, thoroughly hopeless, and profoundly preposterous box" in which "a very flat quilt, covering a very thin mattress, spread like a surgical plaster on a most inaccessible shelf." The "dreary" main saloon resembled "a gigantic hearse with windows in the sides," while glasses and cruet-stands secured in overhead racks "hinted dismally at rolling seas and heavy weather." Dickens's suspicions were soon confirmed. He could not have chosen a worse time of year. A winter crossing — especially a westward one — was virtually guaranteed to be rough. The morning after a particularly bad gale, he awoke to find " . . . the life-boat had been crushed by one blow of the sea like a walnut shell; and there it hung dangling in the air: a mere faggot of crazy boards. The planking of the paddle-boxes had been torn sheer away. The wheels were exposed and bare; and they whirled and dashed their spray about the decks at random. Chimney white with crusted salt; top-masts struck; storm-sails set; rigging all knotted, tangled, wet, and drooping: a gloomier picture it would be hard to look upon."

When *Britannia* finally reached Halifax on the fifteenth night after a storm-tossed crossing, she grounded on a mud bank in a repeat of the previous year's incident. Everyone rushed on deck and confusion reigned, at least initially. Once passengers and cargo were shifted aft to lighten her bow, the steamship was soon off — and straight into more difficulty. *Britannia* dropped anchor in "a strange outlandish-looking nook which nobody on board could recognize, although there was land all about us." Distress rockets and signal guns were fired, but to no avail. A boat was dispatched ashore and returned with the

Charles Dickens, already famous when he sailed to the United States and Canada on a six-month literary tour in 1842.

news they were in Eastern Passage, a narrow, shallow entrance to the harbour unsuited for large ships, "surrounded by banks, and rocks, and shoals." She remained there for the rest of the night and steamed into the main harbour the next morning.

Dickens came out on deck, the "sun shining as on a brilliant April day in England; the land stretched out on either side." Coming ashore, he soon formed "a most pleasant impression of the town and its inhabitants." During the brief stop in Halifax, Howe, now Speaker of the Legislative Assembly, took Dickens in hand, fed and watered him and sat him next to himself for the opening of the new session. Dickens noted the Assembly copied the forms of the "Mother of Parliaments" so closely, but on a much smaller scale, that it was "like looking at Westminster through the wrong end of a telescope."

After seven hours, Dickens continued on to Boston and a six-month literary tour of America and Canada. He opted to return to Britain on an American sailing packet, remarking, "The noble American vessels have made their packet service the finest in the world." *American Notes* sold well, but Dickens's negative embellishment of his voyage on *Britannia* did not escape the critics. One reviewer wrote in the *Illustrated London News*, "Of course this is the mere nonsense of book-making exaggeration, written to kill time and tickle the reader."

Sam's insistence on safety first was attracting more paying passengers to the mail steamers, but they were not coming fast enough and in sufficient numbers. Despite offering the only transatlantic steamship service, his company was losing money. When Sam and Napier negotiated the cost of the ships in the spring of 1839, Sam overstated his case and over-estimated the annual profits of the line at nearly £41,000. While he may have exaggerated this figure to convince Napier and his colleagues to invest in the line, Sam certainly expected to make money. After the first nine months of operation, however, the company had losses of some £15,355.

Combined with his other financial difficulties, the outlook was not only bleak, it was potentially ruinous. Sam considered renegotiating the contract with the government yet again. He approached the government and asked them to double the original annual subsidy to £120,000. In turn, the Treasury asked to see the company's books. Sam willingly obliged. After a Treasury review of the line's figures, the government granted a new contract for £80,000 on September 1, 1841, with the caveat that the company build a fifth steamship (*Hibernia* was launched in 1843). It was an improvement, but not enough to prevent Sam from going bankrupt. In desperation — and probably embarrassment — he turned to his steamship partners for a loan, promising to repay it within two years with interest.

He put up some of his own shares as collateral. They loaned him £15,000 in September 1841; by the next January he had spent it all repaying other debts.

To raise more money Sam sold the house and land at Rawdon where his parents had ended their days, mortgaged his wharves and warehouses in Halifax and secured a £45,000 loan from the Bank of Nova Scotia, in violation of the bank's own regulations. Desperation also drove him to heartlessness. He had his son-in-law and land agent on PEI, James Peters, squeeze his tenant farmers for every possible cent of rent. On the Cambridge estate, where Sam had obtained the right to collect £2,535 in rent arrears, many tenants managed to pay, but others could not. Peters seized their cattle and land throughout 1842 and 1843, and issued leases to new tenants. On one lot in Kings County, about 300 people gathered to reinstate a man who had been legally ejected from his house and farm. Order was restored only when 50 soldiers arrived from Charlottetown.

By the spring of 1842, Sam claimed debts of £130,000, plus mortgaged property of £47,000, against assets of £257,000. Creditors were hounding him. Coincidentally — and perhaps a bit suspiciously — George and William Young ended up as lawyers representing some of his creditors. The members of the Young family were his enemies, intent on seeking not only justice for their clients, but revenge for themselves. The Youngs made it personal. "They have been at different times employed by persons in England," Sam complained, "and they have resorted to every means in their power to injure me by arresting me and heaping costs upon me. You cannot imagine anything more unfeeling than their proceedings — they hesitate at no act if it will put a few pounds into their pocket." Sam even had to flee Britain for Halifax on one of his own ships, slipping past several writ servers.

In addition to his personal debts, the loss for the steamship line for 1842 was £26,400. It marked the lowest point in Sam's finances. He and his partners again asked the Admiralty to raise the subsidy, which they did, and granted another £10,000 a year. Throughout Sam's many

financial troubles, his ships crossed the Atlantic "with regularity almost unexpected and wholly unsurpassed," according to one New York newspaper. Sam's insistence on safety first began to pay off. Moreover, with the demise of his competition, the line became a virtual monopoly and raised its fares unchallenged. Coupled with a general improvement in the shipping business, the company slowly started to turn a profit and work itself out of debt. Gradually, Sam repaid his partners and investors began receiving dividends. The future for the Cunard Line began to look brighter.

Despite Sam's insistence on safety, he was up against a tough opponent in the North Atlantic. No challenge to its harshness went unanswered forever, a fact that remains true today. His steamships had accidents — at least eight groundings besides

A sextant, barometer and telescope, essential requirements for any ship's captain who intended on bringing his vessel safely into port.

Britannia in the first eight years. As well two collisions with smaller vessels sank them and killed eight of their sailors. The most significant accident occurred to *Columbia*, shortly after departing Boston in a thick fog in July 1843. As she approached the Nova Scotia coast, she was pulled off course by a strong current. Enveloped in the fog, her captain could not get his bearings, but imprudently steamed at her full speed of 10 knots. *Columbia* hit and stuck firm on the Devil's Limb, a dangerous reef one and a half miles offshore some 150 miles southwest of Halifax. All attempts to get her off the ledge proved unsuccessful. Her captain — this time prudently — transferred his men and the 85 passengers to a local boat that had appeared on the scene. Waves continued to pound *Columbia*, and eventually she broke up and sank, the first Cunard steamship lost to the Atlantic (*Cambria* replaced *Columbia* in late 1844). The most singular characteristic of all these accidents was that no one on a Cunard ship was killed. It was a fact that continued for Cunard's passengers for 75 years. No other transatlantic steamship line could boast such a record. They all experienced dreadful disasters, several of which caused hundreds of deaths.

Throughout these difficult years, Sam was not alone in running the company. While family looked after business in Halifax and Boston (sons Will and Ned respectively), his senior partners in Britain (Napier, Burns and the MacIvers) remained intimately involved in all aspects of the line, from design through to construction and maintenance, as well as ongoing daily management. Sam's brother Ned retired due to ill health after 25 years of quietly working behind the scenes. Another brother, John, died in the spring of 1844. The next year William Duffus passed away at 83, the same year that Sam's partner David MacIver died.

Sam's daughters Margaret and Ann were married and living in England, leaving only the two youngest girls, Isabel and Elizabeth, still teenagers, at home. Margaret had married William Leigh Mellish in 1843, while Ann had wed army Captain Ralph Shuttleworth Allen in 1844. Sam decided to give up his suite at London's Burlington Hotel and rent a house in the West End, so the girls could live with him during the winter. The girls, however, told him they could not desert their widowed grandmother, the woman who had brought them up after the death of their mother.

While things were finally going well with the steamship side of Sam's business, the same could not be said of some of his other enterprises. He was severely criticized in Nova Scotia for the untendered award of £1,550 a year for eight years from the British Post Office to carry the mail overland from Halifax to Pictou, where it was loaded on *Unicorn* for the run to Quebec. When Canada, which was expected to provide half the amount, refused to subsidize what it considered a purely passenger service, Nova Scotia was stuck with paying the entire bill. Sam was eager to terminate this contract in any case, as well as the steamer service from Pictou to Quebec. The completion of a rail line between Albany to Buffalo meant the mail and passengers destined for Canada could steam directly to Boston, bypassing the two-day coach ride from Halifax to Pictou and subsequent trip to Quebec.

In any case, *Unicorn* was losing money and Sam needed it for the Halifax to St. John's mail run, for which he had just signed the contract. Sam accompanied a British Post Office official to Washington to investigate the possibility of an agreement to transfer Canadian mail across American territory without examination or duty. When such an agreement was signed in 1845, it was largely through Sam's "personal exertions," according to the Halifax newspapers. As a result, the Canadian mail was not taken off at Halifax, Sam sold his fleet of coaches, and *Unicorn* commenced the run to Newfoundland.

All these changes provoked criticism. Joseph Howe fumed about the injustice of "ocean steamers carrying British mail past British provinces to reach their destination through a foreign state." Howe did not blame Sam, who had been instrumental in orchestrating this change, but British colonial policy, made in complete disregard of the colonies' best interests. In particular, Howe was concerned over the growing importance of the railroad, a key factor in a country's development, as the rapid growth of New York since the 1820s had clearly shown. Halifax had no overland communication route with Canada, a shortcoming Howe

Sam's son, William, a director of the company for many years.

wanted to overcome with the building of a railroad.

Such a railroad had been a matter of public discussion for some time, but the cost of laying tracks from Halifax through the New Brunswick wilderness to Quebec was extreme. Sam also supported the railroad. He tried to cushion the blow of *Unicorn*'s withdrawal from the Pictou-Quebec service by stating that he had formed a company with some of his London associates to build a railroad to Quebec, providing the British government financed it. Howe and his fellow Haligonians were cheered by this news, which would ensure their city's place as a key transportation and communication centre.

In an amazing feat, Britannia *was freed from the ice in Boston harbour in 1844 by the combined efforts of men and horses.*

Sam's interest in the railroad was not altruistic. Many of the huge tracts of land that he and his brother controlled in New Brunswick were along the proposed route. A lot of money was to be made providing land for the railroad, and even more to be had in selling land to new settlers once the railroad opened up the country. Two years later, Sam appeared before a government committee investigating railroads as a means of improving immigration to the colonies. He stated that without railroads British North America would never realize its potential. The committee's report was quietly filed and forgotten. The railroad would not come in Sam's lifetime.

The realization that Halifax had been pre-empted by Boston in the transatlantic service finally hit home ("merely as the *touching* place for the Cunard steamers, while Boston was selected as the *stopping* place," as one local newspaper put it). The expected influx of visitors and their trade had gone to Boston, which prospered. The population of the Massachusetts city increased from 85,000 in 1840 to 114,000 in 1845, partly due to steamship commerce.

Bostonians were conscious of the prosperity brought to their city by Sam's steamers. They especially delighted in besting their great rival, New York, served by only one steamship, *Great Western*. New Yorkers had hinted that *Columbia*'s loss was due to sailing from Boston, which forced her to negotiate 450 miles of "rock, ledge, shoal, fog, and narrow intricate channels" along Nova Scotia's coast. Competition between the two cities was so intense that when Boston Harbour froze solid in February 1844, trapping *Britannia* in ice six to eight inches thick, Boston's merchants and citizens united to find a solution. The result was an amazing feat: in two days a 100-foot-wide, seven-mile-long channel cut through the ice to open water, using saws, axes, horse-drawn ploughs and men, paid for with several thousand dollars collected by businessmen. It only delayed the inevitable. Boston eventually ceded pride of place to New York, where the harbour *never* froze.

Meanwhile, back in Halifax, the fine new Halifax Hotel, built to accommodate the anticipated crowds, sat empty. Sam's praises in his hometown were not being sung so loudly. Then there was brother Joe. If his overbearing business practices were not enough, he was being labelled a credit risk in a Halifax newspaper. By now, Sam was no longer active in his brother's firm, although he remained a partner and adviser. During Sam's absences from Halifax, Ned gamely tried to defend his uncle, but neither he nor his father realized how near Joe was to bankruptcy. Through bullying and browbeating, and with support of firms who recognized that if Joe went under he might take them with him, Joe managed to stave off bankruptcy. At this point Henry Cunard, tired of his brother's profligacy, resigned as manager of Joseph Cunard & Company and retired with his wife to Woodburn Cottage, his country estate on the Miramichi.

Joe had created many enemies in establishing his empire, particularly the firm of Gilmour, Rankin and Company. A major dispute erupted concerning improvements to streams running through certain timber leases. Joe promised to erect sluices and clear obstacles as a condition for being granted the leases, but failed to complete the work. Alexander Rankin led the attack against Joe, which resulted in the Colonial Office removing his lease. Additional quarrels followed over timber ownership, trespassing and even the election of Assembly members. The latter disagreement resulted in pitched battles between huge crowds of 500 to 1,000 men during an election campaign. The authorities had to send in troops to restore order.

In the midst of Joe's turmoils, the fortunes of Sam's steamship line continued to improve. His newest ships,

Hibernia and *Cambria*, slightly larger than their predecessors at 1,422 tons and 220 feet long, were built by Robert Steele and equipped with Napier 472-horsepower engines. They carried 155 passengers and 130 tons of cargo, and quickly established new crossing records. They took nine days, 20 hours and 30 minutes outbound to Boston, and eight days, 22 hours and 44 minutes inbound, averaging almost 12 knots. *Hibernia* and *Cambria* continued the line's tradition of austerity, although the odd touch of opulence, such as gilt ceiling mouldings and landscape murals, appeared.

As Sam's steamships took more and more business from the sailing packets, it was inevitable that rival steamship lines would spring up. Early in 1846 (the same year he was elected a Fellow of the Royal Geographical Society), he heard about the first of these. The US Congress awarded a New York group an annual subsidy of $400,000 to begin a steamer mail service between that city and Britain. Sam immediately sailed to London, worried about American

A group of men pauses as they try to break up a log jam on a tributary of the Miramichi. Joseph Cunard had promised to improve streams in the region as a condition of some of his timber leases.

competition and the effect it might have on his ideas for starting a service to New York. He pleaded his case at the Admiralty and Treasury, cleverly combining British national interests with his own. As Sam explained it, American ships "would deprive the Government of half the postage, and deprive me of half the passengers." He asked for an additional £85,000 annually to construct four more ships for a New York run.

Although the Admiralty agreed, the Chancellor of the Exchequer was not so easily convinced and offered £60,000. Sam grumbled, "I would have taken anything almost in order to prevent it," but he thought "it was very unjust" and felt the Chancellor "did it to save money to the country, but he took 25,000 £. a year from me for the good of the country." The new contract specified weekly sailings in the summer and biweekly ones in the winter to the United States, via Halifax to Boston and on to New York on alternate Saturdays, for £145,000 annually.

Docking facilities were arranged at Jersey City, across the Hudson River from the Manhattan docks. Sam's son, Ned, moved from Halifax to New York to become the line's agent. There he married Mary, a daughter of Wall Street financier Bache McEvers in the spring of 1849.

Initially, they lived in a fashionable Fifth Avenue brownstone, but eventually bought property on the highest point of Staten Island and built a fine home. Within a year of the inaugural New York run in December 1848, the company's New York business exceeded the older Halifax and Boston service; by 1850 New York cargoes were nearly double those of Boston.

Ned's younger brother, Will, was the company's agent in Halifax. In December 1851 he married Thomas Chandler Haliburton's daughter, Laura, at Windsor, her father's birthplace. Sam gave them the Brunswick Street house to live in, but Will and Laura later built a magnificent house set in a great park, which they named Oaklands, in Halifax's suburbs. Will, who was appointed the consular agent for France in Halifax, and Laura, a landscape artist of some note, entertained lavishly at Oaklands.

Despite recent criticisms, Sam was admired and regarded in his hometown as one of the most influential men in Britain. "Not infrequently," one Halifax newspaper noted, he was "the trusted counselor and adviser of the highest in the land on important questions pertaining to maritime affairs." Sam had even had an audience with Queen Victoria and Prince Albert, and discussed with them the impact of steam navigation on the British Empire. His own opinion of his achievements was no less than the public's: he was proud of them. In the face of the North Atlantic's known hazards, he had established his steamship line and persevered through one crisis after another. "I originated this service at a great risk and at a time when no other party could be found to undertake it," he declared, resulting in a "beautiful line of commu-

A sketch of the steamboat wharf at Halifax, thought to be the work of Laura Haliburton Cunard.

America *breaking through the ice in Halifax Harbour in 1859, the first time the harbour had frozen in 20 years. Little is known about the history of this watercolour, which is filled with interesting details and was acquired by the Maritime Museum of the Atlantic in 2006.*

nication between the eastern and western world."

America, *Niagara*, *Europa* and *Canada* were built for the run to New York, entering service in 1848. They were 240 feet long and averaged 1,830 tons, 30 per cent larger and more powerful than their predecessors. Even though Napier urged change, they were still wooden-hulled paddlewheelers. Sam would not adopt iron ships with screw propulsion for another decade. At about £90,000 per ship (£50,000 of which was for machinery alone), most of their cost was paid by private capital (although Sam was able to convince the Admiralty to raise his subsidy to £173,340). Their engines were more powerful (around 640 horsepower), with greater steam pressure (18 pounds per square inch, double that of *Britannia*), producing more speed (about 10½ knots per hour). Although more efficient, the larger engines burned more coal, about 60 tons a day.

More power produced more speed, something that always enamoured the paying public. *Canada* quickly established a new eastbound record, while *Europa* set a westbound one. *Niagara* established a different kind of record in the fall of 1849 when she sailed for Halifax and New York with over 160 passengers aboard, the most ever carried by a transatlantic steamer. Two more wooden-hulled paddlewheelers, *Africa* and *Asia*, followed in 1850, each had a speed of about 12½ knots. At 2,220 tons and 265 feet long, they were the largest Cunard ships to date. They differed in design from their predecessors only in the rigging of their sails. The Cunard Line was ready for the new American competition.

Sam may have been ready to face his competitors, but the same could not be said for Joe, whose recklessness and overextension brought him once more to the brink of bankruptcy in 1842. He survived again for the moment, but in 1847 was unable to meet his heavy financial obligations due to depressed economic conditions, irresponsible expansion and strong competition. He finally declared bankruptcy. Panic followed. Hundreds of men depended on him for their livelihood. At his offices on Water Street in Chatham, where many of them lived, angry crowds confronted him, crying "Shoot Cunard!" Never one to back away from confrontation, Joe stood his ground, two pistols prominently protruding from his high boots, and supposedly demanded, "Now show me the man who will shoot Cunard." The crowd backed off.

Joe's bankruptcy threw from 500 to 1,000 people out of work; many left the region in search of jobs elsewhere, especially in Quebec and New England. The bankruptcy also dragged a number of smaller firms down and had an effect on the whole Miramichi timber trade, which took a few years to recover.

Sam returned to Halifax on *Cambria* as soon as he learned of Joe's difficulties. Sam's businesses, many of which operated in some kind of partnership with Joe, were in danger of being overwhelmed by his brother's creditors. Sam soon sorted it out. Even without sufficient funds to cover Joe's debts, he declared all of them would be paid in full. His display of confidence encouraged several merchants in Halifax and Boston to offer their assistance. In two weeks he had enough long-term loans to pay off all the creditors.

Joe left the Miramichi for good in 1850 and moved to Liverpool, England, with his wife and two sons, where he formed a partnership in a ship commission business — with a loan from Sam — acting as a middleman between British buyers and colonial merchants and lumbermen. Joe quickly established himself in Liverpool society, becoming widely known as a genial and kindhearted gentleman of some charm. The relationship between Sam and Joe was never the same afterwards. Although they saw each other frequently, there was never the same degree of closeness as before. Sam could not forgive Joe for dragging down the good Cunard name.

Back in London Sam finally rented a house in Queen's Gate Gardens, Kensington. In the spring of 1850, Isabel asked his consent for her marriage to Henry Holden. "He appears to be a very respectable young man," Sam wrote, "but he has not much money. I must do the best I can for them." He gave each of his daughters an annual allowance of £300, but told them "if you require a further amount from any unforeseen circumstances let me know and you shall have it." He frequently had to follow through on this promise, as none of the daughters married into money. Isabel and Henry wed later that year and moved to Nottingham, not far from her sister, Margaret.

At the time, Jane and her army officer husband, Gilbert Francklyn, were stationed with their children in Colombo, Ceylon (modern Sri Lanka). Since available schooling was unsatisfactory, the three oldest children returned to England to live with their grandfather. Because Sam thought the Kensington house too small for the children, he took out a 10-year lease on Bush Hill House, a country estate in Edmonton, some eight miles north of central London, described as "a capital family residence in the old style, with beautiful timbered grounds and park, entrance lodges, stabling, outbuildings, gardens and appurtenances together about 74 acres." For the next 10 years, Bush Hill House became a second home for Sam's numerous grandchildren. "I shall have so many grandchildren soon that I will not be able to remember them all," he proclaimed proudly in 1850, when there were a dozen. By 1860 the number had grown to three times as many. Bush Hill House was the family's gathering place, the one location where the paths of its far-flung members met. Elizabeth, the only daughter not to marry, joined Sam there when grandmother Duffus finally passed away in 1858 at the age of 86.

Judge Haliburton visited Bush Hill House whenever he was in London to see his publisher, envious of the magnificence Sam's affluence could buy. Haliburton retired from the Supreme Court of Nova Scotia and moved to England in 1856, hoping to emulate the life of an English country squire. He rented a fine villa on the Thames near Twickenham, originally built by George I for one of his mistresses. Later that year, widower Haliburton married well-

Above: The ladies' grand saloon on the Collins Line's Atlantic *in 1850; Right: Portrait of Edward Knight Collins, the founder of Cunard's biggest rival.*

to-do widow Sarah Williams, whom he had first met in 1853.

Sam's first and most serious steamship challenge came from Edward Knight Collins (1802–78), owner of the highly successful Dramatic Line (all its ships were named after actors) of sailing packets. Collins started lobbying the American government for a steamship subsidy as far back as February 1841, a mere eight months after *Britannia's* maiden voyage. His efforts paid off six years later, with the award of a government contract for $385,000 a year to carry the mail — and Congressional direction to beat Cunard.

Collins sold his sailing ships to concentrate on his new line: the New York and Liverpool United States Mail Steamship Company, known simply as the Collins Line. The United States had a long history of steamers built for rivers and lakes, but the country was at a decided disadvantage against British ocean-going steamers. Collins had to design and build his ships and engines virtually from scratch — but he succeeded. His first four steamships — *Atlantic, Arctic, Pacific* and *Baltic* — entered service in 1850. (He explained that since Cunard had already taken the continents, he had to take the oceans). At 2,000 tons and 814 horsepower, they were larger than all but the latest Cunard ships. They also differed in internal and external layout and design. The biggest difference was their opulent public and private passenger furnishings and fit-

The Collins Line Baltic *plows through the North Atlantic. She took the Blue Riband in 1852, the last American ship to do so for 100 years.*

most of all their speed. It was this final factor that drew passengers to the Collins Line, especially Americans. Collins's ships soon established new records for crossing times. In 1851 they averaged seven hours faster to Liverpool and 22 hours faster to New York than the Cunarders.

The American triumph seemed complete, at least to the casual observer. But beneath the surface it was an entirely different story. Their great speed came at a cost in

tings. The contrast with the austere British ships could not have been greater. Such extravagance came at a cost, about $700,000 a ship, nearly 50 per cent more than the original estimate. Nevertheless, the Americans were now ready to go head to head with the British for transatlantic supremacy. Or so the public thought.

William Brown, brother of James, Collins's major investor, was a Liverpool merchant and banker, and one of the largest original investors in the Cunard Line. He regarded his brother's involvement in Collins's new line as folly, but sought to protect both investments. He approached Charles MacIver in early 1849 with a proposal that he hoped would prevent a price war between the two lines. The result was a secret arrangement to set minimum transatlantic fares for passengers and goods, with a guaranteed split of revenues: two thirds to Cunard and one third to Collins. The deal had Sam's blessing. It was kept secret not because it was illegal, but because of the often precarious state of relations between the two countries. The American public and its vociferous media expected Collins to beat out Cunard, not establish a cozy working relationship with his rival.

The Collins steamships were an instant success. People raved about their standard of service, their sumptuousness and

broken, damaged and worn machinery, leading to extensive repairs that might remove any of the four ships from service for months at a time, without warning. Added to these costs was the expense of maintaining high standards of service. Each round trip resulted in an average loss of $17,000. Bankruptcy soon beckoned. Sam was not above gloating that his rival had "discovered that the working expenses amount to double the sum they anticipated."

Even with a continued edge over the competition, or perhaps because of their example, Sam bowed to the inevitable and built his first iron-hulled, propeller-driven ships. Many shipbuilders believed using iron was "contrary to Nature." *Andes*, *Alps* and *Taurus* (the first Cunard ships not ending in "a"), vessels between 1,100 and 1,500 tons, entered service in 1852–53, followed in 1855–57 by *Lebanon*, *Emeu*, *Etna* and *Jura*, between 1,400 and 2,200 tons.

Within two years, Collins went back to the government for an increase to his $385,000 subsidy for 40 trips per year. After interminable debate and extensive lobbying lasting several months, Congress approved Collins's request and raised the figure to $858,000 for 52 voyages. The American eagle was not going to lose to the British lion for a mere lack of funding; in the end the reason was far more tragic.

9 DISASTER & DOMINANCE

On the morning of September 27, 1854, *Arctic*, one of Collins's faster ships (she had taken the Blue Riband from Cunard's *Asia* in 1852), was seven days out of Liverpool, homeward bound with 153 crewmen and 281 passengers, including several members of the Collins and Brown families. On Newfoundland's Grand Banks the steamer entered a dense fog. Captain James Luce tempted fate and continued ahead at her top speed of 13 knots, in accordance with the line's normal practice. Fate soon struck, in the form of the French steamer *Vesta*. Just after noon, *Vesta* ploughed into *Arctic*'s wooden hull, some 20 feet behind the bow, and stuck firm. Ten minutes of reversing engines separated the ships, but the ocean came pouring in through three large gashes in *Arctic*'s hull.

It looked as if *Vesta* had endured the worst part of the encounter and Luce dispatched a lifeboat to help her. Meanwhile, *Arctic* began listing forward and to starboard as jerry-rigged repairs to stop the rush of water proved ineffective. With lifeboats sufficient to carry only 170 of the 434 aboard, Luce ordered full steam ahead for Cape Race, about 60 miles away.

Inset: A linen life vest with 12 blocks of cork stitched inside it; Above: In this painting the Collins steamship Arctic *is shown going down off Cape Race, Newfoundland, on September 27, 1854, after colliding with the French ship* Vesta. *Some 350 aboard perished.*

A nineteenth-century print entitled "Dressing under difficulties" showing one of the many hazards of a storm at sea.

Faced with few options, it was an understandable but disastrous decision, as the ship's forward movement caused more water to gush in through the holes in the bow, snuffing out the lower furnaces. Probably at that point all order and discipline were lost on the ship. The engine room crew deserted their posts and rushed topside, to find a confused, mob-like scene. While some sailors tried to keep manual pumps going, others launched lifeboats. Most lifeboats were filled with sailors, who had pushed women and children out of the way to scramble aboard. Other passengers were kept back at gunpoint.

When *Arctic* went down four and a half hours after the collision, nearly all the passengers were still on the quarter-deck and tumbled into the frigid waters. None of the six lifeboats turned back to pick up those struggling in the water and, at 45 degrees Fahrenheit, the sea soon claimed all but the hardiest. Two lifeboats reached Newfoundland, a third was found by a passing ship, and a few survivors were picked up clinging to bits of wreckage. Over 90 per cent of the passengers died, a scandalous 258, including almost all 109 women and children aboard. The figures for the crewmen, though high, were much better: 60 per cent, some 92 sailors, died.

Victorian society was shocked. This was not the way men were supposed to act in a crisis. For Collins and Brown, the tragedy had a direct personal impact. Collins lost his wife, two children and a brother-in-law and his wife. Brown lost three children, a daughter-in-law and two grandchildren. The conditions under which their lives were lost reverberated across America and Britain; not until the *Titanic* sinking 58 years later would another Atlantic disaster have such an impact.

The Collins Line was down, but not out. At least, not yet. An insurance settlement of $540,000 kept it going, with three ships (now equipped with watertight compartments and more lifeboats) instead of the previous four. The secret arrangement with Cunard, although it involved relatively small sums, also helped. In 1850, Collins received £1,427 from Cunard rising to a total of £21,973 during the next four years. The cartel's real benefit was that it kept prices artificially high and competition out. Even so, the two lines fought to maintain customers and reputations. Cunard began weekly sailings in winter and steamed directly to New York, bypassing Halifax, to compete with Collins. But he could not match the American's speed.

The outbreak of the Crimean war conspired to increase Collins's business. Sam's contract with the British government, like Collins's with the American government, required his ships to be available in the event of war for use as troop carriers. Sam did not wait for the government's call, but directed his ships be made ready for naval use. Eventually, 14 vessels, including eight transatlantic mail steamships, were provided. Collins rushed to fill the gap. His ships established new records during 1855, averaging 28 hours faster to Liverpool and over 31 hours faster to New York than the Cunard Line. With consistent, regular sailings, Collins's ships carried 7,176 passengers across the Atlantic for the year, another record. Collins finally seemed to be succeeding in his avowed aim of "sweeping Cunard from the sea." And he might have, if not for another disaster.

On January 23, 1856, *Pacific* left Liverpool for New York, carrying 45 passengers, 141 crew and 700 tons of cargo. When she did not appear at New York after a normal

A steamship could frequently power its way out of an icefield, where a sailing ship might become trapped, although not all were always able to do so.

winter crossing time of 10 to 12 days, there was no immediate concern. Ships crossing in the winter could become trapped in ice fields — and the ice on the Grand Banks that season was earlier, thicker and farther south than normal. The sighting of a few pieces of wreckage on February 7 was dismissed by the company as inconsequential, "as we think there would have been a much larger quantity of wreck about had it been the *Pacific*." After a month, optimistic observers noted that other ships had been unsighted for longer periods. After three months, most began to accept the inevitable — *Pacific* would never appear and her

The Cunard Line's Arabia *at Napier's Dock, Liverpool in 1853.*

actual fate would never be known. Most speculated she probably foundered off Newfoundland, perhaps the result of a collision with an iceberg, but the mystery was not resolved until 1991. *Pacific's* bow section was found in the Irish Sea, 12 miles off the Welsh coast, only 60 miles from her departure port of Liverpool.

Within 16 months, two Collins Line ships, *Arctic* and *Pacific*, had sunk, killing 536 people. It was more than the American public or government could take. Passengers returned to the slower and safer Cunard line. Reliability was more important than speed. With two of his four ships gone, Collins built a fifth vessel, *Adriatic*, launched in 1856. Few passengers made the one round trip in 1857. Political support for Collins weakened; Congress reduced its subsidy. In a final blow, Collins's partner, James Brown, deserted him. The line's three remaining ships were sold off in 1858 for $50,000, a fraction of their cost. *Adriatic*

became the last wooden paddlewheeler built for the transatlantic service.

Despite the superior shape, speed and service of his ships, Collins was unable to compete with Sam. Collins had overextended himself from the start and was only saved from earlier bankruptcy by the insurance settlement from *Arctic* and *Pacific*. Sam copied several of Collins's more luxurious touches in 1853 in the 285-foot long, 2,400-ton *Arabia*, his last wooden paddlewheeler, capable of averaging 13 knots.

To the British, the whole Collins Line fiasco was simply another example of American youthful brashness succumbing to British maturity and stability. It also seemed that the fabled Cunard luck still held true. In the end, the Collins challenge to Cunard's supremacy on the North Atlantic was the only one that came close to winning. Other American lines followed, but none ever beat the Cunarders as Collins had done, even if only for a brief period. During the last half of the nineteenth century, the United States essentially turned inwards, preoccupied with the Civil War and its aftermath, as well as its expansion to the Pacific, putting into practice the theory of Manifest Destiny. The North Atlantic was left to the British. Sam had won.

Sam's assistance during the Crimean War, although required by the terms of his contract, was nevertheless much appreciated by the British government. His ships had been the most reliable of those called into the Royal Navy's service and a special report outlining his contribution was tabled in the House of Commons. In March 1859, an official announcement in the *London Gazette*, noted that "The Queen has been pleased to direct . . . granting the dignity of a Baronet of the United Kingdom of Great Britain and Ireland unto Samuel Cunard of Bush Hill."

To coincide with his baronetcy, and at Robert Napier's urging, Sam sat for a portrait. Napier presented the oil painting to Sam's youngest daughter, Elizabeth, for her thirty-second birthday. Elizabeth promptly hung it in the dining room at Bush Hill House and sent Napier a thank you note "for a gift that must be valuable to me for its own sake, as well as for the sake of the donor, whose name has been familiar to me from early childhood in connection with much I have heard of science and natural energy and talent."

Haliburton, who became a Tory Member of Parliament that same year and who had long desired such an honour, was impressed with Sam's baronetcy. In private, he thought it was unfortunate that more titles were not given to authors. However, he could be proud of his honorary DCL awarded by Oxford in 1858 for his services to literature, the first colonial to be so recognized. Haliburton's new career as an MP did not lead to any honours; his wit in writing did not cross over into his parliamentary speeches. He was an undistinguished speaker in the House of Commons, a fact reinforced by his gout and a throat ailment.

The two old men saw each other from time to time, sharing Sam's box at the opera or lunching together at the Conservative Club, where their conversation inevitably turned to Nova Scotia. Sam kept Haliburton informed about what was happening in the colony, based on his fre-

An oil painting of an elderly Samuel Cunard, 1849.

quent visits there. Haliburton returned to Nova Scotia only twice after his marriage. They wondered why the province of Canada, created by the 1841 union of Lower and Upper Canada, was surpassing their home province, once so important. The coming of responsible government, instigated by their mutual friend Joe Howe, had not improved the colony's prospects.

Sam suffered a setback in 1853, when a Liverpool firm, followed within two years by Hugh Allan's newly-formed Montreal Ocean Steamship Company (soon known as the Allan Line), received a contract to carry the mails between Britain and Montreal. When the Canadian provinces assumed control of their domestic postal services in 1851, the Canadian (i.e., Ontario and Quebec) government regarded Cunard as a purely British line, and saw no reason to subsidize it, preferring to support the development of a Canadian line. Some mail destined for

Left: The 3,414-ton Persia, *built in 1856, Cunard's first iron ship and regarded as one of the most beautiful of all early Cunarders; Above: Details of the steam engines and paddlewheels of* Persia.

Canada still came through Halifax, for which the Nova Scotia government demanded a subsidy from Canada. Canada promptly refused to pay, an echo of an earlier and similar squabble.

The Allan Line contract was another blow to the dreams of many Haligonians that their city would become one of the world's great ports. Although much of the Atlantic's shipping bypassed Halifax, Sam continued to visit the city of his birth every year. By now the ten-year lease he had taken out on Bush Hill House had run out, and he and Elizabeth returned to Kensington, to a tall, stucco-fronted townhouse in Prince's Gardens.

A debate had been going on among the senior Cunard partners, led by George Burns, over the efficacy of replacing the paddlewheels on the mail boats with screw propellers. Screw propellers now drove Sam's four immigrant ships — paddlewheels and their engines took up valuable steerage space — but he insisted on maintaining paddlewheels on the mail steamers, largely because he felt they looked safer and passengers preferred them. The terms of his mail contract with the Admiralty, dating back to 1839 when screw propulsion was still untested, had never been amended and specified the mails must be carried in paddlewheelers. Sam's ships were the only ones still using paddlewheels on the Atlantic crossing. The other lines running steamships — Inman, Allan, Hamburg-American and North German Lloyd — all used screw propellers for propulsion.

Even after he started using screw propulsion, Sam continued to build additional paddlewheelers. Two more followed *Arabia*, both iron-hulled. *Persia* made her maiden voyage in January 1856 and captured the Blue Riband three months later, holding it until 1862. At 3,400 tons and 360 feet long, *Persia* was the largest ship in the world, as well as one of the most beautiful — but only briefly. The bigger — at 3,800 tons and 380 feet — *Scotia* was launched in 1862, the last and finest of all the Cunard paddlewheelers. *Scotia* incorporated facilities never featured on any ship before, including a bakery, butcher, doctor's office and icehouse, as well as opulence that rivaled anything

Collins had produced. *Scotia* took the Blue Riband from *Persia* in 1862, and held it for five more years in both directions, and several more years westbound.

During the American Civil War, *Persia* and *Scotia* steamed under a neutral flag and became two of the most successful ships in the firm's first 25 years. Many regarded them as the most beautiful paddlewheel steamships ever built. Slowly, between 1850 and 1870, the steamship gradually surpassed the sailing ship, which reached its zenith between 1860 and 1870, and the screw completely replaced the paddlewheel. It took until 1876 before the number of steamships built in Britain exceeded the number of sailing ships. In America, the most renowned

Scotia, *the last and finest of the Cunard paddlewheelers, launched in 1862.*

Top: Designed by Donald McKay, the clipper ship Lightning *set a record that no steamship matched for 35 years; Inset: Nova Scotian Donald McKay became the pre-eminent clipper ship builder of his day; Bottom: McKay's clipper* Flying Cloud *is depicted taking on cargo in New York before departing on her maiden voyage to California in June 1851.*

builder of clipper ships of the period was a Nova Scotian, Donald McKay (1810–80), from the province's South Shore. His ships included *Lightning*, which established a record from Australia to England, *Great Republic*, the largest clipper ever built, and *Flying Cloud*, which set the record for a sailing ship from New York to San Francisco.

China, an iron-hulled, screw-propelled, 2,640-ton steamer entered service the same year as *Scotia*. The two ships had similar lines and provided an opportunity to compare paddlewheel versus screw propulsion. The propeller won easily, producing the same speed but consuming only half the coal. Yet, even the remarkable Isambard Brunel still used old technology in his greatest ship ever, the massive, 22,500-ton *Great Eastern*. Brunel took no chances — the giant ship was driven by both paddlewheels *and* a screw propeller. George Burns believed the product of Brunel's genius would eclipse all other steamships, and he wanted to ensure the Cunard Line's continuing com-

Lithograph of Brunel's Great Eastern, *which was launched in 1858 and was powered by paddlewheels and a screw propeller. For 30 years she was the largest ship in the world.*

petitiveness. Sam was not so sure about *Great Eastern*. In the end, he was right.

Great Eastern's maiden Atlantic voyage in 1860 was disastrous. Riding high in the water, she was caught up in rough seas and rolled and pitched like a nautical roller coaster. Huge waves crashed over her bow, the rudder broke, the paddlewheels washed away and the cowshed overturned, causing a cow to fall through a skylight onto some passengers. The 38 passengers aboard thought they would never reach New York, let alone in a respectable 11 days. The ship's only profitable Atlantic crossing was in 1861, when the British government chartered her to carry 2,500 soldiers and their families to Quebec to reinforce the garrison because of fears of a Fenian invasion. That voyage occurred during fair weather; *Great Eastern* was hopeless in a gale.

Despite a profit of £10,000 on the Quebec voyage, *Great Eastern's* owners went bankrupt and put the steamer up for auction with the firm of Cunard, Wilson & Company of Liverpool, which Joe had originally formed in 1855. Ironically,

Joe's company sold one of Sam's greatest potential competitors. *Great Eastern* was later used to lay underwater telegraph cables, before being broken up in 1889. For his part, Burns conceded defeat to Sam, retired from business and moved to his house on the Firth of Clyde, to be replaced in the firm by his sons John and James.

The rival Inman Line had concentrated on carrying immigrants and made good money at it, so much so that Sam followed suit. In order to turn a profit in the emigrant trade, ships with screw propulsion were required because of the large amount of steerage space needed, space that paddlewheel machinery filled. Sam started a Mediterranean service in the mid-1850s with *Taurus*, and expanded into the emigrant trade by the end of the decade. Four iron-hulled, screw-propelled ships, *Balbec*, *Damascus*, *Kedar* and *Palestine*, were built for this service in 1860, followed by *Olympus* in 1863 and *Aleppo* in 1865. The superior performance of *China* and these other propeller-driven vessels finally led the Admiralty to remove the paddlewheelers-only restriction on carrying the Royal Mail. No more paddlewheelers were built for the Cunard Line.

By 1860 Sam owned one-sixth of all the land on Prince Edward Island, some 212,885 acres stretching from one end of the small colony to the other. He was its largest absentee landlord. The Colonial Office regarded him as an expert on the Maritime provinces and the landlords' spokesman. In an attempt to resolve land ownership disputes in the colony, the Island's legislature requested the creation of a special land commission. British authorities consulted Sam about all appointments to the commission.

The commissioners recommended the extension of an earlier Land Purchase Act to the whole Island, funded by the British government, with a system of compulsory sale with prices set by arbitrators. Sam learned of this proposal in 1861 and he immediately wrote to the Colonial Secretary, the Duke of Newcastle, to object to farms being valued by arbitration. He claimed, "as one of the largest proprietors in the island," that although the maximum purchase price was 20 years' rent, arbitrators might instead decide that a fair price was only two or three years' rent, subjecting the owners to massive losses. When the Island's assembly attempted to implement the commission's recommendations, Newcastle vetoed it.

Many Islanders rightly blamed the absentee owners for the British government's failure to provide funds to buy out the landlords and for not enforcing compulsory sale of their holdings by arbitration. Sam and other proprietors, keenly aware of how disappointed the Islanders would be by this latest failure to resolve the land issue, made their own offer after consultation among themselves. They offered their land at the equivalent of 15 years' rent, to be open for a five-year period from May 1862. The Island's Executive Council promptly rejected their offer.

Shortly afterwards, a Tenant League was formed on the Island; its agitation often made it difficult for the owners to collect their rents. In February 1863, Sam wrote to the Colonial Office claiming, "There is no tenant on the Island who cannot pay his rent, if he industrious and sober," noting "while the agitation is kept up by designing people, rent will not be paid nor money laid up to purchase farms; time is wasted and money spent in attending political meetings." Later that year, an official delegation from the Island journeyed to England to request implementation of the land commission's recommendations. The Colonial Office forwarded their request to Sam, who again objected to the terms, specifically of forgiveness of rent arrears and the proposed terms of sale.

The colonial delegation disputed many of Sam's contentions and asked for some compromise from the landlords. The Colonial Office, in a clear indication of Sam's influence, listened to his demand that neither the imperial government nor the Island legislature should interfere "with our property, in any manner different from that in which private estates in England should be dealt with." As a result, Sam's holdings remained his property until after his death, when they were sold to the Island government.

Following a mild heart attack, Sam retired in 1863. He was 76 years old. His son Ned became a senior director, dividing his time between Britain and America. Sam made what was to be his last trip home in the summer of 1864, staying with Will and Laura at Oaklands. He spent a few days at the Brunswick Street home he had built for Susan 50 years earlier, now in a decidedly less fashionable part of town. He also visited one of his few business peers still alive — and still active — Enos Collins, now 90, at his estate, Gorsebrook, near Oaklands. Collins had been in partial retirement since he left the Executive Council in 1840, watching his investments, but mainly spending his days in the seclusion offered by his great estate. Talk of more change was in the air, speculation about a possible union of the three Maritime colonies. That summer the Canadians invited themselves to a conference in Charlottetown, pushing aside the idea of Maritime union for a greater union of all the British North American colonies. Collins and several other merchants feared the effect such a union would have on their businesses and strenuously opposed the idea, along with Joseph Howe. The old man severed his lifelong allegiance to the Conservatives over the issue, and gave his financial backing to Howe and the anti-Confederation league.

Howe had been temporarily removed from local politics with his appointment as imperial Commissioner of Fisheries in 1862, established as a result of Britain's 1854 Reciprocity Treaty with the United States. Howe had first lobbied for a provincial appointment in 1842 — in clear contrast to his criticism over the years of public officers who took so much of the colony's revenue. He had repeated his requests several times, especially after 1855 when he sought an imperial appointment. Most Maritimers joined Collins and his fellow merchants in opposition to the idea of what the Canadians were calling "Confederation." They objected to a central government far inland presuming to dictate policy to the coastal colonies. To many, absorption by America was preferred.

Sam returned to Britain on *Scotia*, his last paddlewheeler and one named for both his home province and the country that had built his ships and their engines. Despite the fact that they were expensive to operate and lost money, *Scotia* and *Persia* were the most popular ships on the North Atlantic, with a loyal following of wealthy travellers. As Sam crossed the ocean that summer, he was the acknowledged master of the North Atlantic. Other steamship lines were in operation, but none equalled the line he had started.

The American Civil War (1861–65) — which saw the Confederacy use several fast paddlewheelers as blockade runners — affected Sam's highly profitable immigration business and brought much of the United States shipping to a standstill. Sam happily filled the gap. Two-thirds of all U.S. mail destined for overseas was carried on his ships.

Back in Britain, Sam's health began to fail that fall. A small man, he became thin and seemed to shrink. In December, he suffered an acute attack of bronchitis and took to his bed to recover. His brother Joe, 65, was having health problems of his own. He had a heart attack in Liverpool after Christmas. Sam was determined to visit him, in spite of the protestations of Elizabeth and his doctor. He had seen little of his brother during the past few years and felt he had to see

Samuel Cunard's house at 257 Brunswick Street as photographed in 1870.

Joe to assure him there were no hard feelings over Joe's massive debts, debts that Sam was still repaying for years.

Sam was ready to go when a letter arrived from Joe's wife saying he was making good progress and should be completely recovered in a month. Less than three weeks later, on January 16, 1865, Joe suddenly dropped dead in the ornate drawing room of his Liverpool residence, in the midst of a few friends. Sam never recovered from the shock of his brother's unexpected death.

The estate of Joseph Cunard, who once ran much of the Miramichi region of New Brunswick like a private fiefdom, amounted to a paltry £14,000. Nothing was available to pay down Joe's debts, which remained the responsibility of S. Cunard & Company in Halifax. It took six more years, until 1871, to eliminate them completely. Joe was a colourful, larger-than-life character who had played a key role in the commercial development of the Miramichi region, but his business failures adversely affected the economy of the area for many years.

When Sam experienced another attack of bronchitis in early April, his family and friends knew he could not last much longer. His final attack occurred on Sunday, April 23, at two o'clock in the morning. The doctor was called and stayed by his bedside for the rest of the day and Monday. By Tuesday, he seemed to be recovering, although he slept fitfully. He had not had the chance to make proper amends with his brother, and now his long-ago fight with George Burns bothered him. On Friday, April 28, he asked Ned (by now, both sons were with him) to write a letter for him to the Scotsman. Ned obliged, the letter went off and Sam dozed more calmly that afternoon. He died at six o'clock, with his sons at his side. Before he passed away, during a wakeful moment, he said, "I have been dreaming about your dear mother." He was buried in the Brompton Cemetery, 37 years after and half a world away from his wife. Thomas Chandler Haliburton followed his friend three months later, on August 27.

Back in Nova Scotia, the Halifax merchants and the rest of the colonies' residents never got to decide their future; the governments of Nova Scotia and New Brunswick decided to join the Canadian colonies in 1867 without putting the question to the electorate (only tiny Prince Edward Island decided against it, at least until 1873). Largely because Premier Charles Tupper did not consult the people on their wishes for colonial union, Howe returned to politics and formed an anti-Confederation party. It won 18 of the 19 Nova Scotia seats in the first federal election in September 1867, 80 days after Confederation came into effect. Armed with such clear support, Howe sailed to England in February 1868 to lobby for a repeal of the British North America Act. But British parliamentarians, happy to be rid of the many bothersome problems caused by separate colonies, were not prepared to revisit the issue.

Howe returned to Nova Scotia and realized that he had no choice but to make the best of a bad situation. He negotiated better financial terms for the province with Sir John A. Macdonald, but only on condition that he join the federal cabinet to indicate his unequivocal support for Confederation. He did so, becoming President of the Privy Council. He was regarded by some of his supporters as a turncoat.

Howe died four years later, in May 1873, a mere three weeks after being sworn in as his province's lieutenant-governor. No one had cheered him on his return to Nova Scotia. One of his biographers has noted, "It was the tragedy of his homecoming that killed Howe," while a friend claimed he died "of a broken heart, so deeply wounded by those who had been his friends and should have judged him as stirred by higher motives than anything personal to himself."

Cunard's transatlantic mail contract was up for renewal on December 31, 1867 and the British Post Office was anxious to reduce its annual subsidy to the company, which was £170,000 at the time. The Cunard Line had no interest in maintaining the Liverpool to Boston route via Halifax with a reduced subsidy and dropped Halifax as a port of call for its mail steamships, but continued its weekly mail service to New York with a subsidy of £80,000. The new Inman Line received the contract to deliver overseas mail to Halifax for £10,000 annually.

On December 21, 1867, *Cuba* sailed out of Halifax. It was the last Cunard ship to see the great harbour for nearly 50 years. Her departure was a blow to the economic development of the city and the region. Cunard's other business interests followed suit, leaving a retail coal outlet as the only remnant of the great company in Halifax.

Sam's estate was valued at £350,000 (about $1,750,000), not that great a fortune even for the time. By comparison, his sometimes business partner, the astute Enos Collins, who died in 1871 at 97 years of age, left a fortune estimated at least $6,000,000, making him possibly the richest man in British North America. Each of Sam's six surviving daughters received £20,000, with the remaining £230,000 divided between Ned and Will. Sam's Prince Edward Island lands were sold for $257,933.30 in July 1866 to help pay for his daughters' legacies.

Conclusion
— The Cunard Legacy

Sam's death marked the beginning of a period of decline for the steamship line he founded. By 1870 four other companies were carrying more passengers across the Atlantic than Cunard, most of them immigrants. Without Sam's presence to hold things together, no one seemed ready to exert the firm control the company needed. Robert Napier had essentially retired by the late 1860s, respected throughout Europe for his work, but strangely never honoured in Britain, even though he was known as "the father of Clyde shipbuilding" and had done more than anyone else to make the Clyde the greatest shipbuilding river in the world.

Napier passed his shipbuilding firm to his son, John, whose first major ship had been the paddlewheeler *Scotia*, a fast, beautiful vessel, but a money loser. He also built *China* in 1862, the first Cunard screw-propelled ship designed for the Atlantic with space to carry immigrants. However, John was not the builder his father had been, and when Cunard ordered the construction of *Cuba* two years later, he turned to the firm that built the Inman Line's immigrant ships.

Of Sam's other partners, the surviving MacIver brother, Charles, was old and ill. John and James Burns were inexperienced, at least for the time being. Sam's son Ned — now Sir Edward — may have inherited his father's title, but he did not inherit either his father's judgment or his knack of inspiring others with his vision. He spent far too much of his time in New York to be able to run the company as Sam had. These deficiencies became moot four

One of Cunard's pre- and postwar "Big Three," Mauretania *held the Blue Riband longer than any other ship. She is pictured here off Staten Island in New York Harbour in 1931.*

years after Sam died, when Ned succumbed to a sudden heart attack in the American city. Ned's eldest son, Bache, automatically inherited the title, but as he was only 18 years old, the responsibility of running the company was given to Will, Sam's only other son and the company's agent in Halifax.

Will sold Oaklands and moved to London with his family, passing the management of the company's Halifax office to his cousin John Morrow and his nephew George Francklyn. Although he had been the line's agent, Will knew nothing about running a steamship company. However, he was an astute investor and built up the inheritance that Sam had left him, and that his brother Ned had left his children. Will was also clever enough to listen to others and encourage their ideas.

Faced with competition from Thomas Ismay's new White Star Line, which launched its first steamer in 1870, ideas were very much needed. The Cunard Line, sticking rigidly to its inherent conservatism, was rapidly becoming out of date. It continued to emphasize reliability and dependability, while other lines boasted of their ships' facilities. Cunard ships

William Cunard's extensive estate, Oaklands, overlooking Halifax's Northwest Arm, ca 1870.

remained simple and unadorned, a continuing reflection of Sam's original vision. In contrast, the White Star ships could be considered the first of the modern luxury liners, boasting compound engines, promenade decks, wide saloons, bridal suites and even more mundane improvements such as replacing candles with oil lamps.

All the Cunarders could boast of was their unrivaled safety record, never having lost a passenger — or even a letter. No other line even came close. American humourist Mark Twain once noted, "It is rather safer to be on board their vessels than on shore," adding they would "not take Noah himself as first mate till they had worked him up through all the lower grades . . . . When a thing is established by the Cunarders, it is there for good and all, almost. Before adopting a new thing the chiefs cogitate and cogitate; they lay it before their purveyor, their head merchant, their head builder, their head engineer, and all the captains in the service . . . . Then if the new wrinkle is approved it is put into the regulations."

The Inman Line eventually lost six ships, including *City of Glasgow*, which simply disappeared with 480 passengers and crew in 1854, and *City of Boston*, which sank off Ireland in 1870, with the loss of 177 souls. The Hamburg-American line fared only slightly better, when *Austria* burned at sea in 1858, killing 470 passengers and crew. It was the White Star Line, however, that set an unenviable record. On April 1, 1873, *Atlantic* was making for New York, when her captain changed course to refuel at Halifax. In the middle of the night, still thought to be "about 48 miles from land," *Atlantic* ran straight onto an offshore ledge near the tiny coastal village of Prospect and grounded. Pounded by giant waves, which defeated most attempts by local fishermen to rescue those on board, *Atlantic* eventually broke up on the rocks. Only a few people, mostly crewmen, were saved; 545 were killed. It was the worst shipwreck the Atlantic had ever witnessed. Thirty-nine years later, and not that far away, another liner set a new and as yet unbroken record: In 1912 the *Titanic* went down off Newfoundland after colliding with an iceberg, taking 1,513 souls with her. Also a White Star Liner, *Titanic* was

Print of the wreck of the Atlantic *off Nova Scotia in 1873 — the worst nautical disaster before* Titanic *sank in 1912.*

owned by Bruce Ismay, Thomas's son.

Over time, the Cunard Line slowly regained its prominence. In 1874 it initiated a popular 13-week "circular voyage" through the Mediterranean and Black seas, the forerunner of the modern cruise. In 1878, the company's Atlantic and Mediterranean fleets amalgamated to become the Cunard Steam-Ship Company. At the same time, the Burns, MacIver and Cunard families, each holding a third of the firm's stock, decided to take the company public, partly because it became impractical to run such a big business privately. A new house flag was designed to help attract buyers on the London Stock Exchange. The

Scottish Cross of St. Andrew was replaced with a crowned British lion rampant, holding the globe between his front paws. When the stock went on the market in 1880, eager buyers snapped it up.

Will Cunard was a hard worker who remained a director of the company for several years. He and his wife, Laura, lived in various elegant houses in and near London, with a winter home on the French Riviera near Nice. Will's son, Ernest, followed as a director, the last Cunard to serve on the company's board. Sir Bache Cunard, Ned's son, never entered the family business and was content to live the life of a country gentleman in an English Georgian cas-

Top: Servia, *launched in 1881, was Cunard's first steel ship and the first to be lit by electricity; Above:* Oregon, *launched in 1884, met disaster two years later off New York City, when she collided with a wooden schooner and sank. Fortunately, the famous Cunard luck held and everyone aboard was rescued.*

tle, where he pursued his hobby of silversmithing, and a Staten Island estate. His American-born wife, Maud, was a famous Edwardian hostess. Their one daughter, Nancy, was a leading member of London's post-First World War literary set and a writer of some note.

By the last quarter of the nineteenth century, Cunard ships were innovators rather than followers. *Servia*, launched in 1881, was the first steel ship of the line (steel ships had been built as early as 1865) and the first to be lit by electricity, perhaps the most welcome of all improvements on liners — even more than running water. *Servia* made 16.9 knots on her trial run. With her sister ship, *Aurania*, launched in 1883, the Cunarders were firmly reinstated as the pre-eminent transatlantic line, a position they maintained despite the loss of another ship, Cunard's second peacetime disaster.

Oregon, over 7,300 tons and 500 feet long, was launched in 1884 and took the Blue Riband the same year. Approaching New York with about 900 passengers and crew just before dawn one day in March 1886, *Charles H. Morse*, a 500-ton, 150-foot wooden sailing schooner, heavily laden with coal, inexplicably rammed the steamer's port side amidships, bounced off her iron hull and struck again, punching two 20-foot holes in her side.

Oregon stopped and began to drift as seawater poured in through the huge gaps. *Morse* was nowhere to be seen, probably having sunk.

Panic set in among the passengers, but was immediately quelled by the steady actions of the captain and crew. Women and children were first loaded into lifeboats and then transferred to a pilot boat that appeared on the scene. A passing German steamer took the remaining passengers and crew. Between nine and 10 hours after the collision, *Oregon* went down in 80 feet of water, the top of her mainmast still visible. Everyone on board was saved, as well as some of the mail. It was Cunard's last peacetime sinking and allowed the company to continue its boast that it had never lost a life at sea.

Strictly speaking, the claim was not quite true. While Cunard had never lost a life due to shipwreck, passengers had been killed on the company's vessels. The first recorded instance occurred in May 1867, when a rogue wave swept over *China* and killed prominent Halifax banker James Cogswell. Between 1888 and 1902, six steerage passengers were killed at sea. The worst single incident occurred in October 1905, when a giant wave swept over *Campania*'s foredeck, just as she rolled to leeward. Five steerage passengers were washed overboard and drowned.

Campania and *Lucania* were launched in 1893, the firm's first twin-screw liners, and the first without sails and with refrigeration. At 12,950 tons and 601 feet, with 10 times the interior space of the original 1840 Cunarders, they sported huge raked funnels instead of the little stovepipes of earlier ships. They were the most luxurious Cunard ships to date. They were also the fastest, propelled at a service speed of 21 knots by 30,000-horsepower engines, the most powerful yet built, enabling them to break the North Atlantic's 20-knot barrier. *Campania* and *Lucania* set new transatlantic records of five and a half days in each direction, the epitome of nineteenth-century ocean travel. It took 415 crew members, eight of them women, to see to the ship's 2,000 passengers, ranged in three classes. In 1901, Marconi conducted wireless telegraphy experiments aboard *Lucania*, making ship-to-shore com-

The 13,000-ton Campania, *which entered service in 1893, was one of Cunard's first twin-screw liners.*

Above: Postcard of Lusitania *docked at Liverpool's Landing Stage, 1910s; Below: A silver souvenir spoon and gold brooch in the shape of a ship's wheel, both from* Aquitania *and part of the Maritime Museum of the Atlantic's collection of Cunard memorabilia.*

munications possible.

The period between 1900 and the start of the Second World War has been referred to as the golden age of steam, an era of large, luxurious liners crossing the ocean, carrying the rich and famous of the day. Steam turbines driving triple screws made their first appearance on the Cunarder *Carmania* in 1904. In 1907 two ships that made history in completely different ways were launched. *Lusitania* and *Mauretania* were the biggest (nearly 32,000 tons and 762 feet) and fastest (25 knots service speed) ships on the Atlantic run, and quickly became the most popular. They were the first ships to employ quadruple screws.

The British government heavily subsidized their construction to enable them to compete with the faster German liners and provided an annual subsidy, providing they could maintain an average speed of 24½ knots and were available to the country in time of war.

Lusitania gained permanent recognition in one of history's most infamous acts, when the German submarine *U-20* torpedoed her 10 miles off the Irish coast on May 7, 1915, in what has been termed the war's single most barbaric act. Some 1,198 passengers and crew out of the 1,959 on board died. While the rest of the world reeled from the shock, the German Kaiser ordered a national day of celebration. Ten other Cunard liners were sunk during the war.

Despite these tremendous losses, Cunard returned to its dominant position after the war. To replace *Lusitania*, it was awarded the German liner *Imperator*, which was promptly rechristened *Berengaria*. Oil-fired engines had replaced coal-burning ones just prior to the First World War, raising steam pressure to produce greater speeds, while reducing engine room gangs significantly. *Berengaria* joined *Aquitania* and *Mauretania* to become Cunard's post war "Big Three."

Cunard began to build a fleet of 12 intermediate-sized liners, which entered service in the early 1920s. At the same time, it changed the homeport for its big express liners from Liverpool — which it had used since *Britannia*'s maiden voyage in 1840 — to Southampton, because of the draught required by the larger vessels. Liverpool remained the homeport for the intermediate-sized ships.

In the opinion of many, *Mauretania* was unmatched by any other steamship in history. While others may have exceeded her in one or two qualities, none equalled her combination of speed, beauty, technology, moneymaking ability, durability and just plain luck. She could carry up to 2,165 passengers in three classes and quickly set new crossing records in both directions, holding the Blue Riband until 1929, a remarkable 22 years. After the First World War, *Mauretania* became the steamship of choice for rich Americans visiting Europe and the watchword for the sophisticated traveller. *Mauretania* remained in service until 1935, when she was broken up, her fittings and furnishings auctioned off. Some of them ended up in a pub in Bristol, where they may still be seen today.

When Sir Bache Cunard died in 1925, his title went to his brother, Gordon, followed by Sir Gordon's son, Edward.

When Sir Edward died in 1962, the title passed to Will's side of the family, a somewhat fitting tribute to his long years of work for the company. Will's great grandson became Sir Henry in 1962 and held the title briefly until his death in 1973, when Henry's brother, Guy, inherited it. Sir Guy Alick Cunard was the seventh and last Cunard baronet. He died unmarried and childless in 1989 (see Appendix).

The Cunard *Queens, Mary* and *Elizabeth*, both the originals and their reincarnations, have become the best-known super liners of all time. The first *Queen Mary*, designed in the 1920s, was the first ocean liner over 1,000 feet, the first to reach 80,000 tons and the first designed to cross the Atlantic on a five-day schedule. She was longer, wider and had twice the displacement of the world's largest warship at the time, the battlecruiser H.M.S. *Hood*. Although laid down in 1930, *Queen Mary* was not ready to enter service until 1936, long delayed due to the Great Depression.

Queen Elizabeth quickly followed her sister. Due to make her maiden voyage in 1940, she had to flee a Britain under assault from the German Luftwaffe for New York before that happened. In New York her final outfitting was

Mauretania's first class music room and lounge.

completed, now in wartime gray. Together, the *Queens* provided invaluable wartime service to the Allies, each able to transport a division of troops or more at one time on most of the world's oceans. By the end of the war, between them they had carried well over 1,500,000 soldiers. In Winston Churchill's opinion, "The *Queens* helped to win the war in Europe by at least a year."

The Great Depression had an immediate effect on all passenger lines, as travel for pleasure was one of the first luxuries to disappear with money in short supply. With the steamship companies facing extinction, massive government intervention was soon recognized as the only way to save them. In Britain, the Chancellor of the Exchequer, Neville Chamberlain, was prepared to help, but only on the condition that the Cunard and the rival White Star Line merged, a long-held goal of his.

In desperation, many passenger lines had already turned to "cruises to nowhere" in an attempt to generate income. Cunard and other companies even started the "Booze Cruise," a three-day excursion from New York or Boston to Halifax and back, whose sole purpose was to circumvent Prohibition. Sometimes fares were as little as $5, but the lines made money on alcohol sales. Once outside territorial waters, liquor flowed like water. Such cruises only delayed the inevitable and in January 1934 the Cunard-White Star Line came into existence. The immediate result was recommencement of work on Hull 534 — launched six months later as *Queen Mary*.

After the war, *Queen Mary* was restored to her pre-war glory, while *Queen Elizabeth*'s was achieved for the first

QE1 *arrives in New York in June 1945 carrying 14,000 Canadian and American troops.*

time. They entered commercial service in 1947, shuttling between Southampton and New York at 27 to 28 knots, with a call at Cherbourg. *Queen Mary* carried a maximum of 1,957 passengers. *Queen Elizabeth* carried 2,233. The healthy financial situation created by the *Queens* enabled Cunard to buy out the White Star interests and revert to its original name in 1949. By the mid-fifties, the *Queens* had substantially assisted in solidifying Cunard's grip on the transatlantic passenger trade. Along with 10 sister

Queen Mary, *flagship of the merged Cunard and White Star lines, in a 1930s poster.*

ships, four of them (*Saxonia*, *Ivernia*, *Carinthia* and *Sylvania*) on the Canadian run, they carried one-third of it. The *Queens* remained the most popular — especially with the celebrities of the day — and the most profitable.

Inevitably, however, the jet airliner took business away from the *Queens*. Within a year of the first commercial flight across the Atlantic in October 1958 it captured 63 per cent of all transatlantic passenger traffic. By 1961, the two *Queens* began to lose money. In an attempt to stop

the loss, and after an expensive and extensive refit to *Queen Elizabeth*, Cunard turned the *Queens* into cruise ships. It was an unfortunate decision, which resulted in even greater drains on the company's finances, a prelude to its near demise.

In 1967 the hammer fell. Cunard announced the withdrawal of *Queen Mary* from service at the end of the summer season, to be followed by her sister at the end of the 1968 season. Worse was to come, as staff and ships were laid off. Suddenly, the great company that Sam Cunard founded was on its knees. *Queen Mary* sailed from New York on September 22, 1967, on her last transatlantic passenger voyage.

Of the several bids received for the ship, some of which would have kept her cruising, the southern California city of Long Beach submitted the highest — $3,450,000 — and acquired the aging steamliner. After some initial difficulties, including financial losses, the venerable *Queen Mary* now sits as part of an attractive tourist site, which includes Howard Hughes huge wooden flying boat, the *Spruce Goose*, fulfilling the roles of hotel, convention centre, shopping complex and museum.

The fate of *Queen Elizabeth* was much sadder. Initially, she ended up in Port Everglades, Florida, intended as the east coast equivalent of her older sibling. After two years of neglect, Hong Kong businessman C.Y. Tung outbid several Far Eastern scrap yards. He intended to turn her into a floating university and cruise ship. After some refitting in Hong Kong harbour, five fires broke out simultaneously in different locations in *Queen Elizabeth* in January 1972. Heavy structural damage resulted from the weight of water pumped in to extinguish the fires. The *Queen Elizabeth* capsized the next day, settling on the bottom in 45 feet of water at a 45 degree angle. Her charred corpse was described by a newspaper as "a mess of unrecognizable, tangled steel." Arson, perhaps the result of bad relations between China and Taiwan, was suspected, but never proven. Tung initially planned to refloat the wreck and repair the damage, but it was too great. Within two years, she was cut up and carted away by a Japanese salvage firm, a sad and inglorious end to a proud *Queen*.

Cunard had started planning for a replacement for *Queen Mary* — a 75,000-ton liner known as Project *Q3*. It had to suspend work on the project in 1963 due to the downturn in the firm's finances. Two years later, another smaller design, Project *Q4*, was proposed, and her keel was laid on the Clyde in 1965. *Queen Elizabeth 2*, popularly known as *QE2*, was the result, launched in September 1967 and outfitted for both transatlantic crossings as well as tropical and around the world cruises. Disastrous sea trials, which resulted in severely damaged turbines, delayed her maiden voyage until May 1969.

QE2 was an instant success with the travelling public, but not such a success financially. Operations barely broke even, adding to Cunard's downward fiscal spiral. Eight of its last 10 years finished in the red and caused Cunard's board of directors to put the company up for sale. Trafalgar House PLC, a diversified firm whose assets included travel and leisure industries, bought the firm in August 1971. For the first time in 131 years, the line that Sam Cunard had founded was no longer an independent corporation.

Trafalgar House nearly destroyed what had once been a proud steamship company, the standard by which all others were measured. It immediately sold off *Franconia* and *Carmania*, leaving only *QE2* and two new, much smaller ships to carry on the Cunard name. The two small ships never found their niche and both were sold off by 1976. Trafalgar House then acquired two 17,500-ton ships in 1976–77, and operated them with limited success in the Caribbean.

Instead of building its own ships, the company picked up the cast-offs of others and lost some of its original identity in the process. Even *QE2* was losing her identity. An extensive refit in 1972 altered her exterior appearance and made several questionable interior changes. Additionally, the old Cunard standards of shipboard service dropped considerably, replaced by an informality and casualness that many regarded as an unacceptable loss of dignity. Revenues fell further.

In 1982, as Trafalgar House considered adding two inter-mediate-sized ships to its fleet, the Argentinean invasion of the Falkland Islands interrupted their plans. As it had for her illustrious *Queen* predecessors, the British government requisitioned *QE2* as a troop carrier. After an extensive and hurried refit to convert her to a warship, including painting her gray, *QE2* sailed from Southampton for the Falklands with a complete infantry brigade aboard, as well as several support units, some 3,000 soldiers in all. Once they were safely disembarked in the Falklands, *QE2* underwent another conversion, to a hospital ship, and carried 640 injured British servicemen back to Britain. A tumultuous homecoming in mid-June was exceeded only by the return of the entire British task force at the end of July.

With the war over, Trafalgar House acquired two 24,000-ton cruise liners (*Vistafjord* and *Sagafjord*) from Norwegian America Cruises, which entered Cunard service in 1983. In October 1986, *QE2* made the last steam-powered passenger transatlantic crossing in history, on her way to a £100,000,000 refit in Germany, which replaced her steam turbines with diesel-electric power. The Age of Steam on the North Atlantic was over.

So, almost, was Trafalgar House. In 1996, it was taken over by the Kvaerner Group, a Norwegian conglomerate with no desire to spend the money to upgrade the cruise fleet it had inherited as part of the deal. As speculation centred on who might buy the troubled line, Cunard announced it was moving its corporate American offices from New York City, where it had been since the mid-nineteenth century, to offices near the Miami International Airport in Florida to take advantage of various incentives.

Among the many potential buyers, it was Miami-based Carnival Corporation, parent company of Carnival Cruise Lines, the largest in the world, that acquired a majority (68 per cent interest) in Cunard in 1999. It purchased the remaining 32 per cent in 2000. Although Carnival was fully aware of the bad shape Cunard was in, fears that another cruise line might acquire Cunard and stiffen the competition forced their hand. One of the first acts of the new owners was an $18,000,000 refit of *QE2* in 2000, many elements of which harkened back to the great Cunard liners of the past.

Queen Mary 2 *sailing past the Statue of Liberty and up New York's Hudson River.*

Despite these improvements, *QE2* will eventually retire, probably before she reaches her fortieth birthday in 2009.

At about the same time, *Vistafjord* was renamed *Caronia 3*, in obvious homage to one of Cunard's most popular ships, and given a completely new, "British" look (*Sagafjord* had been sold in 1996). The most dramatic news of all was that Carnival's revitalization of Cunard would include the construction of the largest and most luxurious true ocean liner ever built. She was to be known as *Queen Mary 2*, or *QM2* for short.

Construction began on *QM2* in January 2002 in Saint-Nazaire, France. Due to expected labour difficulties with Britain's intransigent trade and shipping unions British yards were avoided. *QM2* was completed in December 2003, a 150,000-ton, 1,132-foot giant, built at a cost of $800,000,000. In a concession to British indignation, Carnival confirmed that *QM2*'s captain, officers, flag and homeport would be British. The new ship made her maiden voyage in January 2004. In September 2004, *QM2* docked at Halifax, not far from the wharves where Sam got

his start in the shipping business, 164 years after his *Britannia* sailed into the same harbour to begin a worldwide revolution in transportation and communication. The steamship line that Sam had founded so many years ago was back on top again.

Despite the impact that Samuel Cunard had on global transportation and communication, his presence in the city of his birth was barely recognized. A street, a junior high school, an apartment building (on the site of his Brunswick St. house) and a couple of plaques were all that honoured him. In 1997, well over 100 years after his death, he was inducted into the Nova Scotia Business Hall of Fame. Nationally, in 2000, a *Maclean's Magazine* poll selected him as one of Canada's top 25 most influential citizens of all time. In 2004 Canada Post honoured him with a postage stamp, part of a two-stamp set (the other stamp pictures Sir Hugh Allan).

Finally, in 2006 two projects honouring Cunard were unveiled in his home town. The first one was announced in the spring of 2006. It is a major renovation of the

QM2 was berthed in Halifax on October 3, 2005, the day the creation of a statue in Cunard's honour was announced for the waterfront.

harbour's seawall, where cruise ships dock. The cornerstone of a multi-year, multi-million dollar redevelopment of the seawall area, which opened that summer and will eventually include arts facilities, shops, a hotel, open markets and a streetscape, is a 45,000 square-foot combined home port and events centre named after Samuel Cunard.

The second project took much longer to come to fruition. For many years, Halifax lawyer John Langley, the founding director and chairman of the Cunard Steamship Society, a non-profit organization dedicated to the preservation and protection of the history of Samuel Cunard and his legacy sought proper recognition of the city's greatest son. His idea was to erect a statue of Cunard somewhere on the waterfront. Through the efforts of the Halifax Foundation, under the chairmanship of former Nova

Scotia lieutenant-governor Alan Abraham, Langley's dream was finally realized when the Samuel Cunard statue project was announced in October 2005, appropriately aboard *QM2* while she was docked in Halifax. The project cost $275,000 ($75,000 of which came from the Cunard Line). The memorial, created by local sculptor Peter Bustin, was unveiled in the fall of 2006.

These long overdue acknowledgements and recognition of Samuel Cunard's roots and his legacy overlook Halifax Harbour, where the little man with the big ideas started his remarkable revolution so many years ago.

APPENDIX
THE CUNARD BARONETCY

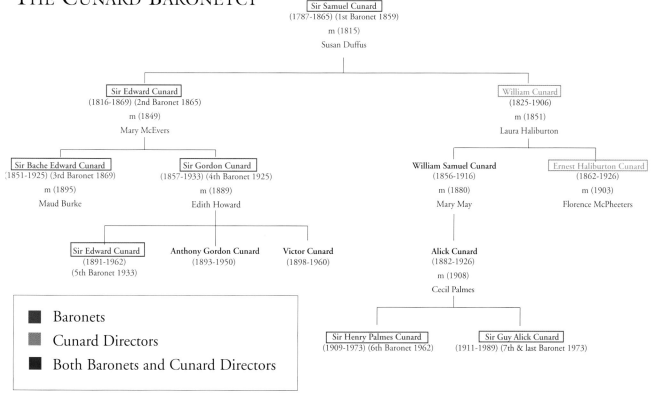

Sir Samuel Cunard
(1787-1865) (1st Baronet 1859)

m (1815)

Susan Duffus

Sir Edward Cunard
(1816-1869) (2nd Baronet 1865)

m (1849)

Mary McEvers

William Cunard
(1825-1906)

m (1851)

Laura Haliburton

Sir Bache Edward Cunard
(1851-1925) (3rd Baronet 1869)

m (1895)

Maud Burke

Sir Gordon Cunard
(1857-1933) (4th Baronet 1925)

m (1889)

Edith Howard

William Samuel Cunard
(1856-1916)

m (1880)

Mary May

Ernest Haliburton Cunard
(1862-1926)

m (1903)

Florence McPheeters

Sir Edward Cunard
(1891-1962)
(5th Baronet 1933)

Anthony Gordon Cunard
(1893-1950)

Victor Cunard
(1898-1960)

Alick Cunard
(1882-1926)

m (1908)

Cecil Palmes

Sir Henry Palmes Cunard
(1909-1973) (6th Baronet 1962)

Sir Guy Alick Cunard
(1911-1989) (7th & last Baronet 1973)

■ Baronets
▨ Cunard Directors
■ Both Baronets and Cunard Directors

ILLUSTRATION SOURCES AND CREDITS

Abbreviations: LAC: Library and Archives Canada; MMA: Maritime Museum of the Atlantic; MMNN: Mariners' Museum Newport News; NMM: National Maritime Museum; NSARM: Nova Scotia Archives and Record Management; PANB: Provincial Archives New Brunswick; PEM: Peabody Essex Museum; SML: Science Museum London Front cover: Courtesy Cunard Line; top left NSARM. Back cover (top to bottom): Charles Chichester, LAC C-150424; Photo: Gary Castle, MMA; William John Huggins MMNNLP140. Preliminary material: p.1, photo courtesy of Cunard Line; p.3, Cunard Line poster, *The Great Liners* (Time-Life Books 1978). Introduction: p.5 (top), *The Liners: A History of the North Atlantic Crossing* (Allen Lane, 1976); p.5 (bottom) Unknown artist, published by George Isham Parkins, LAC C-000984; p.6, after an engraving by Day & Haghe, *Samuel Cunard* (Ryerson 1928). Chapter 1: p.7 (top), Artist: Thomas Birch; p.7 (bottom), original postage stamp; p.9, Artist: Henry Sandham, LAC C-000168; p.11 (top), Artist: J.E. Woolford; p.11 (bottom), Photo: Julian Beveridge; p.12, *The Whalers* (Time-Life Books 1980), p.13 (top) Photo: Keith Vaughan; p.13 (bottom) NSARM; p.14, MMA. Chapter 2: p.15, *Cunard and the North Atlantic 1840–1973* (MacMillan 1975); p.16 (top) Photo: Gary Castle, MMA; p.16 (bottom), Artist: attributed to George Tobin, LAC C-150490; p.17, Mary Evans Picture Library; p.18, Philadelphia Maritime Museum; p.19, *Halifax: Cornerstone of Canada* (Windsor 1985); p.20 Artist: A.C. Mercer; p.21, Artist: Joseph Partridge, NSARM; p.22, LAC C-003372. Chapter 3: p.23, Engraver: James Thomson, LAC C-011567; p.24 (left) Artist: Charles Chichester, LAC C-150424; p.24(right), Photo: Gary Castle, MMA M54.42; p.25 (top), *Pictorial History of Ships* (Octopus 1977); p.25 (bottom), original postage stamp; p.26, Metropolitan Toronto Library Board; p.27, Artist: Charles Lawrence, MMNN QO582; p.28 *Pictorial History of Ships* (Octopus 1977); p.29, Maryland Historical Society; p.30 (top), *The Age of Sail* (Formac 2001); p.30 (bottom), PANB. Chapter 4: p.31, Artist: attributed to Tinqua, PEM 0246; p.32 (top), Nova Scotia Historical Society Collections; p.32 (bottom), Bowater Mersey, Liverpool, NS; p.33, Berry-Hill Galleries; p.34, Photo: Keith Vaughan; p.35 (top): The Collection of the Dartmouth Heritage Museum; p.35 (bottom), *River of Dreams* (Nimbus, 2002); p.36 (top), NSARM 1979-147.766; p.36 (bottom), Photo: Gary Castle, MMA; p.37, Artist: William Smyth Maynard Wolfe, LAC C-122336; p.38, *The Sailing Ship* (Roydon 1984); p.39 and p.40, The Collection of the Dartmouth Heritage Museum. Chapter 5: p.41, Artist: J.E. Woolford; p.42 (left), New York Public Library; p.42 (right), NSARM photos 40231, p.43, Photo: Keith Vaughan; p.45, Artist: James Pattison Cockburn, LAC C-012649; p.46 (top) Culver Pictures; p.46 (centre) Public Records Office, London; p.47, LAC C-021-843; p.48 (top), Artist: Charles William Jefferys, LAC 1970-188-2093 W.H. Coverdale Collection of Canadiana; p.48 (bottom), *Seven Centuries of Sea Travel* (Leon Amiel 1973); p.49, *The Great Liners* (Time-Life Books 1978), p.50, Artist: Fanny A. Bayfield, LAC C-005796; p.51, Artist: J. Gordon, Dalhousie University Killam Library. Chapter 6: p.53 (top) *The Great Liners* (Time-Life Books 1978); p.53 (bottom), Artist: Joseph Walker, SML 10265968; p.54, SML; p.55 (top) Artist: S. Walters, LAC C-000003; p.55 (bottom), NSARM photos; p.57, The Metropolitan Museum of Art; p.58; *Cunard and the North Atlantic 1840–1973* (Macmillan, 1975), p.59, PEM. Chapter 7: p.61 and p.63, Glasgow University Archives and Business Records Centre; p.64 (top), *The Age of Sail* (Formac 2001), p.64 (bottom), G.P.O. Records Room; p.65 (top), Liverpool City Libraries; p.65 (bottom), Cunard Line; p.66, William John Huggins, MMNN LP140; p.67, Artist: Alexander Cavalie Mercer, LAC C-013769; p.68, Cunard Line; p.69, Booklet: *Cunard Steamship Co, Ltd, Over Eighty Years of Trans-Atlantic Travel, 1840–1922*, MMA 73.117.36; p.70, *The Great Liners* (Time-Life Books 1978). Chapter 8: p.71, MMNN; p.72, Artist: William Beatham, Province House; p.73, Artist: Fitz Hugh Lane, PEM; p.74, *Dickens* (Harpercollins 1991); Photo: Gary Castle, MMA; p.77, Photo: William Notman Collection, NSARM 50699/N-432;p.78, NMM; p.79, PANB; p.80, Artist: attributed to Laura Haliburton Cunard, LAC C-117697; p.81, Artist: Avery, Photo: Gary Castle, MMA; p.83, *The Great Liners* (Time-Life Books 1978); p.84, Collection of the New York Chamber of Commerce. Chapter 9: p.85 (top) Newfoundland Museum, St. John's, Newfoundland; p.85 (bottom), Walter Lord Collection; p.86, *Ocean Liners* (New Burlington 1977); p.87, North Wind Picture Archives; p.88, *Pictorial History of Ships* (Octopus 1977); p.89, Artist: Albert G Hoit, NSARM; p.90 (top), *The Great Liners*, (Time-Life Books 1978); p.90 (bottom), Frank O. Braynard Collection, p.91, Photo: Gary Castle, MMA; p.92 (top), *Pictorial History of Ships* (Octopus 1977); p.92 (inset), The Metropolitan Museum of Art; p.92 (bottom), PEM; p.93, *Pictorial History of Ships* (Octopus 1977); p.95, James Rogers Collection, NSARM. Conclusion: p.97, Edvin Levick; p.98, William Notman Collection, NSARM; p.99, MMNN; p. 100 (top), Photo: Gary Castle, MMA; p.100, *QE2* (Norton, 1993); p.101, Artist: R.H. Neville-Cumming; p.102 (top), postcard; p.102 (bottom), Photo: Gary Castle, MMA; p.103, *The Liners: A History of the North Atlantic Crossing* (Allen Lane 1976); p.104, World Wide Photo; p.105, Cunard Line poster; p.107, photo courtesy Cunard Line; p.108, photo courtesy Halifax Port Authority.

BIBLIOGRAPHY

Appleton, Thomas E. *Ravenscrag: The Allan Royal Mail Line*. Toronto: McClelland & Stewart, 1974.

Arnell, J.C. *Steam and the North Atlantic Mails: The Impact of the Cunard Line and Subsequent Steamship Companies on the Carriage of Transatlantic Mails*. Toronto: Unitrade, 1986.

Babcock, F. Lawrence. *Spanning the Atlantic*. New York: Knopf, 1931.

Bassett, John M. *Samuel Cunard*. Toronto: Fitzhenry & Whiteside, 1976.

Bathe, Basil W. *Seven Centuries of Sea Travel: From the Crusaders to the Cruises*. New York: Leon Amiel, 1973.

Beck, J. Murray. *Joseph Howe, Vol I, Conservative Reformer, 1804–1848*. Kingston & Montreal: McGill-Queen's University Press, 1982.

Bolger, Francis W.P. (ed). *Canada's Smallest Province: A History of P.E.I.* Charlottetown: PEI Centennial Commission, 1973.

Braynard, Frank O. & William H. Miller, Jr. *Picture History of the Cunard Line, 1840–1990*. New York: Dover, 1991.

Brinnin, John Malcolm. *The Sway of the Grand Saloon: A Social History of the North Atlantic*. New York: Delacorte, 1971.

Butler, Daniel Allen. *The Age of Cunard: A Transatlantic History 1839–2003*. Annapolis, MD: Lighthouse, 2003.

Butler, John A. *Atlantic Kingdom: America's Contest with Cunard in the Age of Sail and Steam*. Washington, D.C.: Brassey's, 2001.

Charlebois, Dr. Peter. *Sternwheelers & Sidewheelers: The Romance of Steamdriven Paddleboats in Canada*. Toronto: NC Press, 1978.

Coleman, Terry. *The Liners: A History of the North Atlantic Crossing*. London: Allen Lane, 1976.

Cook, Ramsay (gen ed). *Dictionary of Canadian Biography Online*. Various entries. www.biographi.ca.

Croil, James. *Steam Navigation and Its Relation to the Commerce of Canada and the United States*. Toronto: William Briggs, 1898.

Cuthbertson, Brian. *Voices of Business: A History of Commerce in Halifax 1750–2000*. Halifax: Transcontinental, 2000.

Deeson, A.F.L. *An Illustrated History of Steamships*. London: Spurbooks, 1976.

Davies, Richard A. *Inventing Sam Slick: A Biography of Thomas Chandler Haliburton*. Toronto: University of Toronto Press, 2005.

Dickens, Charles. *American Notes*. New York: St. Martin's, 1985.

Fox, Stephen. *Transatlantic: Samuel Cunard, Isambard Brunel, and the Great Atlantic Steamships*. New York: HarperCollins, 2003.

Fraser-MacDonald, A. *Our Ocean Railways or, the Rise, Progress, and Development of Ocean Steam Navigation*. London: Chapman & Hall, 1893.

Fry, Henry. *The History of North Atlantic Steam Navigation with Some Account of Early Ships and Shipowners*. London: Sampson Low, Marston, 1896 (facsimile reprint, London: Cornmarket, 1969).

Grant, Kay. *Samuel Cunard: Pioneer of the Atlantic Steamship*. London & Toronto: Abelard-Schuman, 1967.

Griffin, Peter W.M. *Paddle Steamers*. London: Hugh Evelyn, 1968.

Haws, Duncan. *Ships and the Sea: A Chronological Review*. New York: Crowell, 1975.

Hyde, Francis E. *Cunard and the North Atlantic 1840–1973: A History of Shipping and Financial Management*. London: MacMillan, 1975.

Langille, Jacqueline. *Samuel Cunard*. Tantallon, NS: Four East, 1992.

MacMechan, Archibald. *Samuel Cunard*. Toronto: Ryerson, 1928.

Maddocks, Melvin. *The Great Liners*. Alexandria, Va.: Time-Life, 1978.

_____. *The Atlantic Crossing*. Alexandria, Va.: Time-Life, 1981.

Manny, Louise. *Ships of Miramichi: A History of Shipbuilding on the Miramichi River, New Brunswick, Canada, 1773–1919*. No. 10 in the Historical Studies Series of the New Brunswick Museum, 1960 (reprint, Saint John: Miramichi Books, 2000).

Martin, J.H. & Geoffrey Bennett. *Pictorial History of Ships*. London: Octopus, 1977.

Maxton-Graham, John. *The Only Way to Cross*. New York: Macmillan, 1972.

_____. *Queen Mary 2: The Greatest Ocean Liner of Our Time*. New York: Bulfinch, 2004.

Miller, William H., Jr. *The Last Atlantic Liners*. London: Conway, 1985.

Miller, William H., Jr. *Picture History of the Queen Mary and the Queen Elizabeth*. New York: Dover, 2004.

Payne, Abraham Martin. "The Life of Sir Samuel Cunard, Founder of the Cunard Steamship Line, 1787–1865." *Collections of the Nova Scotia Historical Society*. Vol XIX, 75–91.

Payzant, Joan M. & Lewis J. Payzant. *Like a Weaver's Shuttle: A History of the Halifax-Dartmouth Ferries*. Halifax: Nimbus, 1979.

Raddall, Thomas H. *Halifax: Warden of the North*. Halifax: Nimbus, 1993.

Robertson, Ian Ross. *The Tenant League of Prince Edward Island, 1864–1867: Leasehold Tenure in the New World*. Toronto: University of Toronto Press, 1996.

Roche, T.W.E. *Samuel Cunard and the North Atlantic*. London: MacDonald, 1971.

Rowland, K.T. *Steam at Sea: A History of Steam Navigation*. Newton Abbot: David & Charles, 1970.

Rutland, Jonathan. *All Colour World of Ships*. London: Octopus, 1978.

Spicer, Stanley T. *The Age of Sail: Master Shipbuilders of the Maritimes*. Halifax: Formac, 2001.

Warwick, Captain Ronald W. *QE2*. New York: Norton, 1993 (2nd ed).

Watt, D.S. & Raymond Birt. *The Queen Elizabeth: The World's Greatest Ship*. London: Winchester, 1947.

Woods, Shirley E., Jr. *The Molson Saga, 1763–1983*. Toronto: Avon, 1984.

INDEX